YOURS TILL DEATH

Civil War Letters of John W. Cotton

John W. Cotton

From a picture presumably made during the War

Courtesy Mrs. J. D. Cotton and Miss Myrtice Cotton

YOURS TILL DEATH

Civil War Letters of John W. Cotton

Edited by

LUCILLE GRIFFITH

ASSISTANT PROFESSOR OF HISTORY
ALABAMA COLLEGE

UNIVERSITY OF ALABAMA PRESS

ISBN 0-81735043-8 (alk. paper)

Preface

The "lost man" of Southern literature is about to be found, the leading article in *The Southern Packet* recently announced.[1] For years it had been the colonel, the hoop-skirted belle, the dashing cavalier in a setting of moonlight, magnolias, and mint julips, that writers both North and South fictionized. It was a starry-eyed unreal and nostalgic type of literature about a type of folk that never numbered more than a small fraction of the people of the region. More recently there came a reaction and the nation was fed on *Tobacco Road, Sanctuary,* and much other sociological writing about perverts and degenerates, the shiftless and characterless, which infuriated loyal Southerners because it did not represent a "true picture" of their beloved South. Most of the people *they* knew did not fall into either class.

There seem to be signs, however, which indicate that the lost man— the "nice people"—is about to be found. The short stories as well as longer novels of Peter Taylor, Frances Gray Patton, James Street, Haydn's *The Time is Noon*, Rick's *The Hunter's Horn*, all deal with the "middle men," the lawyers, business men, and teachers who live in the average towns and the familiar countryside.

There is a forgotten man in Southern history, too, especially in the period before the Civil War. He is the vast majority of people who lived in most parts of the South, some four or five million of him in 1860. For lack of a better word historians have called him the yeoman farmer; he belonged neither to the landed slave-owning aristocrats nor to the po' whites. He was a land owner and proud of his independence; he often owned two or three slaves with whom he worked in the field, but more often he and his sons did their own farming; he usually saw eye to eye with the planters on the slavery question; he was a Democrat in politics but was more familiar with Jackson than Jefferson; he belonged to one of the evangelical sects and had a strict code of conduct; and he exhibited what has become known as "typical American" interest in his children and concern over his own small domain.

This class of people has not been completely ignored by the his-

1 *The Southern Packet*, IV, 5, Ashville: Stephens Press, May 1948.

torians. Pioneer work in this field has been done by Owsley,[2] Shugg,[3] and Weaver.[4] By studying official records, especially the census records of 1850, they and others have come to the conclusion that land owning was widely distributed; that in a few such areas as the Tidewater, the Black Belt, and the Delta large plantations were the rule, but in most other sections the middle group of land owners, those owning from 250 to 500 acres, was much larger than formerly thought and in many areas formed the backbone of the community.

Planters kept elaborate records, farm journals, and diaries, but the yeoman farmer either wrote little or what he did write has not been preserved. There is, it must be admitted, very little glamor in the life of a man of few acres and no slaves, a man of small importance in affairs of state even if he is honest and home loving. Source material is not entirely lacking, of course, but with relatively few exceptions, it is fragmentary. It is a happy incident, therefore, when a considerable body of material on this group of people comes to light. Such are the letters of John W. Cotton.

"For the first time in life [I] take my pen in hand to write you a few lines to let you know I am well." Thus begins the first letter of John W (eaver) Cotton to his wife, Mariah. This was written on April 24, 1862; the letters continue at irregular intervals until February 1, 1865. Sometimes there are three a week, more often one a week, and a few times more than a month elapses between letters. In all there are 156 from him to his wife, four from his wife to him, and a few (not included in this book), from members of Mrs. Cotton's family who still lived in Georgia.

John W. Cotton and his wife, Mariah Hindsman Cotton, were born in Coweta County, Georgia, near Grantville, in 1831 and 1833, respectively, and came to Coosa County, Alabama, in late 1853 or 1854. In 1862, when the husband joined the army, they had seven children; one, Nancy Hanner, died on July 18, 1862, and another, James Weaver, was born on April 28, 1864.[5]

---

[2] Frank L. Owsley, *Plain Folk of the Old South*, Baton Rouge: The Louisiana State University Press, 1949.

[3] Roger W. Shugg, *Origins of Class Struggle in Louisiana*, Baton Rouge: The Louisiana State University Press, 1939.

[4] Herbert Weaver, *Mississippi Farmers, 1850-1860*, Nashville: Vanderbilt University Press, 1945.

[5] He purchased his first land in Coosa County from his father, Cary Cotton, on August 29, 1853, while he still lived in Coweta County, Georgia (*Record of Deeds* [Coosa County] H. Old Series, p. 468). Their son John Michael was born in Coosa County March 30, 1855 (family Bible in the possession of Mrs. Arah P. Stanley).

On the surface the Cotton letters are another collection of personal experiences during the war. Mr. Cotton was a private in the cavalry the entire time he was in service. He enlisted April 1, 1862, at Pinckneyville and was paroled May 25, 1865, at Talladega.[6] He was first in Company C (Captain M. G. Slaughter's company) 5th Battalion, Hilliard's Legion, Alabama Cavalry; later (December 30, 1862) this battalion was consolidated with the 19th Regiment Confederate Cavalry.[7] In these two organizations he saw action in East Tennessee, around Murphreesboro and Chicamauga and in the Dalton-Atlanta campaign. The 10th was in Wheeler's last raid, moving north as far as Saltville, Virginia. Its last stand was at Bentonville, North Carolina; it surrendered with the army of Joseph E. Johnston.[8] Because there was absolutely no censorship, Mr. Cotton told many things like numbers engaged and plans for future movements that would have been entirely prohibited in later wars.

A closer examination will show that the letters are more than one man's view of the war. Mrs. Cotton with seven small children, the oldest not yet twelve years old, was left at home to run the farm. While she seems to have been a resourceful person about most things, she was quite dependent on his advice about running the farm, for such matters as what crops to plant, when to plant the grains, the best time and place to market the products, and many other things that need to be answered in the man's absence. Again and again she wrote, "Send me some advice." This advice, some times specific and at other times general, gives an insight into the running of a small farm. The Cottons did not own any slaves but hired one Manuel, who belonged to a neighbor. He stayed with the family all the time the head of the house was away and, although repeated attempts were made to buy him, he was not for sale.

The farm of John W. Cotton was near Mt. Olive in Coosa County, Alabama; the tract is just off the road between Hanover and Mt. Olive, which was a post office in the 1860's. This farm had 285 acres of unimproved land, presumably timber and pasture land, and 65 acres of improved land. It was valued at $1,200. In 1860 the agriculture census shows he owned 2 horses, 1 mule, 4 milk cows plus 17 head

6 Major General Edward F. Witsell, Adjutant General, to Lucille Griffith, April 5, 1950. Union records show he was paroled as a prisoner of war.

7 "Tenth Reg't Confederate Cavalry," typed MS in Department of Archives and History, Montgomery, Alabama.

8 W. Brewer, *Alabama: Her History, Resources, War Record and Public Men from 1540 to 1870*, Montgomery, Alabama, Barrett and Brown, 1872, p. 693.

of "stock" cattle and 2 work oxen, 30 sheep and 28 swine, all valued at $750.[9]

The Cottons were general farmers, as the size of their land holding would indicate; the census reports list the products of the farm as wheat, corn, oats, peas and sweet potatoes in addition to the live stock mentioned above. Wheat may have been a new crop to the family—at least it was a very important one. In the very first letter he says "I reckon I wont come home til the wheat gets ripe" and ends by asking his wife to write soon how "things are going on" and especially how the "wheat is doing." Not once, either in the official records or the letters, is cotton mentioned and we may assume they raised none of the staple.

It is to be remembered these were letters written by a man to his wife with no thought of publication; in all probability he would be amazed that any importance would be attached to them. There is the typical soldier's griping about food, mud, drunk officers and no furloughs; a resourcefulness that is typically American; a love of home and his children and an interest in their development; an honesty and uprightness that is refreshing; and through them all a pathetic homesickness and longing for "this unholy mess" to be over so that he may enjoy peace at home again and "fondle his children at his knee and watch them frolick about."

The letters are published without change in spelling, capitalization or punctuation. Because they have not been handled much, they are in remarkably good condition.

John W. Cotton came home when the war was over but lived only until December, 1866, dying when he was thirty-five. Family tradition says he came home in the rain with measles, from which he never recovered. No one knows how the letters became the posssions of his daughter Virginia, "little Ginny." After marrying Johnnie Monk and rearing a family she died and her personal things were put in a small leather-covered trunk which was not opened until her husband died years later. In the division of family keepsakes, her daughter, Mrs. Ludie Porch of Arab, Alabama, got the letters. They now belong to Mrs. Arah P. Stanley of Verbena, Alabama, daughter of Mrs. Porch and therefore great granddaughter of John W. Cotton.

Thanks go to a number of people for their work on this publication: to Dr. Hallie Farmer, head of the Social Science Division at Ala-

[9] *Eighth Census*, 1860, Agriculture, Coosa County, Mt. Olive District Schedule 4, p. 13.

bama College, who encouraged the project from the beginning and was generous with office help; to students who have helped with the typing; to county officials in Coosa County, Alabama, and Coweta County, Georgia, but above all to Mrs. Arah P. Stanley, who owns the original letters and has worked with the editor step by step. Together with the editor she has interviewed kinfolk, hunted through moldy court house records, and climbed fences and briar patches looking for cemeteries. It has been a labor of love for both Mrs. Stanley and the editor.

Lucille Griffith

Alabama College
Montevallo, Alabama
July, 1950

Contents

1862

Alabama Montgomery Aprile the 24 1862

Mariah Cotton[1] dear wife for the first time in life take my pen in hand
to write you a few lines to let you no that we are all well William
lessley[2] has been sorta puny but he is better he is down in town garding the yankes there is 744 yankeys here in a old ware house and we
have to help gard them we have been examined and received and
they say our horses will be praised today and our legion will also be
organized today I would bee very glad to see you and the children I
am very well satisfyed concidering the way I left home If I could see
you and the children[3] when I wanted to see you I could make out very
well we are camped two miled south east of montgomery we received
our bounty money[4] yesterday it is uncertain how long we will stay
here I dont recken I will come home til wheat[5] gets ripe unless we git

---

[1] Mariah Hindsman Cotton was born in Coweta County, Georgia, on May 17,
1833, and married to John Weaver Cotton on February 7, 1850 (family Bible in
possession of Mrs. Arah P. Stanley). Mrs. Cotton was seventeen and her husband
nineteen at the time of their marriage. They moved to Coosa County, Alabama,
sometime between 1853 and 1855. In 1853 John W. Cotton purchased his first land
in Coosa County from his father, Cary Cotton. The transaction was made in Coweta
County, Georgia. A son, John M., was born in Coosa County in 1855. (*Federal
Census* 1860, Schedule 1, Free Inhabitants in Second Subdivision of the County of
Coosa, State of Alabama, p. 48).

[2] William Lessley, 26, a neighbor, who was also enlisted in Captain Martin G.
Slaughter's Company. *Muster Roll of Captain M. G. Slaughter's Company of the
Cavalry Battalion of Hilliard's Legion of Alabama Volunteers in the Service of the
Confederate States.* MS. in Department of Archives and History, Montgomery, Ala-
bama, (Cited hereafter as *Muster Roll*).

[3] In 1862 Cotton had seven children: Ann T. "bornd" December 16, 1850, John
Michael Cotton (Bud) born March 30, 1855, William Cary (Bunk) born April 21,
1856, Nancy Hanner (Little Cricket) February 3, 1858; Jefferson Davis (Babe) born
March 11, 1859; Andrew C. L. T. (Sweet) April 22, 1860; Virginia Francinia (Ginny) born December 18, 1861, family Bible. Ann is the only one he ever calls by
name; for the others he uses nicknames.

[4] A bounty of fifty dollars was granted to all privates who enlisted for three
years or the duration of the war (James M. Matthews, [ed.] *The Statutes at Large
of the Confederate States of America*, Richmond, R. H. Smith, Printer to Congress,
1864 [Cited hereafter as *Statutes*] 1, 223. December 11, 1861).

[5] This is the first mention of the wheat crop, which, judging by the frequent
references to it, must have been very important to Cotton. Corn, oats and rye
were other grains also raised on the farm (*Eighth Census*, 1860, Agriculture, Coosa
County, Mt. Olive District, Schedule 4, p. 13).

orders to leave if we get orders to march I wil come home sooner I
would bee glad to bee there and see how things are going on and
look around a little rite to me and tell me how my wheat is doing
and how things are going on nothing more at present but remain your
affectionate husband til death John W Cotton to Mariah Cotton

Montgomery Camp Mary Alabama   May 1 1862
Mariah Cotton   Dear Wife I take my pen in hand to drop you a few
lines to let you no that I am tolerable well I have had a very bad cola
but I am better I am not atall sick but feel sorta bad I hope these lines
will find you all well and I hope you have got more reconciled about
my leaving you and the children I think if you could see these yankeys
that we have to gard down here you would yap, whip them or dye on
the battle field[6] I have hope to gard them for days and nights there is
over eight hundred of them in all some of them wants to get home
very bad and others dont seem to care mutch about it I would bee very
well satisfyed if I could see you and the children when I wanted to I
want to see you all very bad and I would bee glad to here from you
all for I have not herd nary word from you all since I left home I
would bee glad to here how my wheat was comeing on and how manuel[7] was comeing on with his crop we here down here that wheat is all
ruined with the rust if it is I may bee at home in about two weaks
but if it is not I dont guess I will come until it gets ripe the most of
our men is at home now we here that the yankeys have taken neworleans[8] some of the people here are very badly scared and are moveing
out there families and they are halling oft the cotton they say that our
men burnt two hundred bails for oald howel nose we are doing very
well now we got plenty to eat and nothing to do but to gard the yan-

6 Cotton began the war with a typical soldier's disdain for the enemy which
continued for some months. See August 1, 1862. This attitude changed, however,
by November and morale was lowest in the winter months. About December each
year he heard rumors of peace being made "about spring." For example see December 1, 1862. (Unless otherwise stated dates of letters are from J. W. Cotton to
his wife).

7 Manuel is a slave, apparently belonging to a Mr. Brown, who was hired by the
Cotton family to do the farm work. Each year before the first of January, Cotton
began to worry that his wife would not hire him for the coming year. They even
tried to buy him but he was not for sale. October 25, 1863; November 29, 1863.
The Cottons did not own any slaves but were willing to buy one.

8 New Orleans was not occupied by the Union Forces until May 1, the day this
letter was written, but Admiral David Glasgow Farragut had reached the city from
the mouth of the Mississippi River on April 25.

keys our company[9] has been received and our horses praised and we have got our bounty money but we have not got our saddles yet nor I dont no when we will get them we cant drill any until we get our saddles for a heap of our men have not got no saddles I want you to rite to me and tell lis to rite too dock[10] rote a letter yesterday bet I dont no what he put in it nothing more at present but remain your affectionate husband til death   John W. Cotton

Alabama Montgomery County May the 5 1862
Mariah Cotton Dear wife I again take the opportunity to rite you a few lines to let you no that I am well and doing well we get a plenty to eat but it is badly Cooked we had nothing fit to Cook with but we have bought some things but not enough yet we draw meal flour pickle pork pickled beef and some times fresh beef rice sugar molasses and soap I am very sorry to here that the wheat has got the rust so bad I am glad to here that manuel is trying to do comething and getting along so well but I was a heap gladder to here that you were all well except bad coles there is several of our boys complaining but none of them bad off I never wanted to see any body as bad as I want to see you and the children I could do very well if I could see you and the children every time I wanted to but I cant help studying about you all If I could see you and talk with you I could tell you of a great many things that has passed since I left you I think if nothing happens I will bee at home about the 20 of this month the most of our men

---

[9] Captain Martin G. Slaughter's Company, Hilliard's Legion, Co. C, Calvary Battalion. *Muster Roll.* Hilliard's Legion was consolidated into the 10th Confederate Cavalry at Murphreesboro, December 30, 1862. ("Tenth Regiment Confederate Cavalry", typed MS in Archives, Montgomery).

[10] Dr. Andrew C. L. Hindsman, a brother of Mrs. Cotton. Sometimes he is called "Bud" but more often "Dock". Lis is Sarah E. Hindsman, his wife, sometimes called Lizzie. She is "from the North", presumably from New York City. (Mrs. Sarah E. Hindsman to Mariah Cotton, December 31, 1860).

It is presumed that Dr. Hindsman was a graduate of the University of the City of New York. Among the letters there is an announcement of "the course of lectures and recitations at Aylett's Medical Institute, of 107 East Fourteenth Street, New York", with a list of the graduates of March 5, 1860. Hindsman is among them. Most of the 119 graduates were from the Southern states: 13 from Alabama, 12 from Georgia, North Carolina, 26. One graduate was from Bermuda, another from "W. T." P. A. Aylett, M. A., M. D. was from Alabama. Research thus far has revealed little about the school. While the announcement would lead one to think it was a separate institution "under the immediate patronage of the Faculty of the University", the information from the New York Academy of Medicine is that Dr. Aylett, a 1845 graduate of the University of the City of New York, did private tutoring under the sanction of the college (letter to Lucille Griffith, May 1, 1950).

is gone home now but the captain says they shant go no more I could
have come two but I thought as I could not come but once that I
would wait a while I recived a letter from you this morning dated the
29 of Aprile for the first dock got a letter from lis last saturday that
was the first time I had herd from you I recken you herd that the
yankeys had taken neworleans we are still garding what yankeys we
have got here yet one of our men killed one of them the other day for
disobeying orders one of our sodiers belonging to our legion shot another the same day and the day before one of our men got drounder
in the river[11] Mariah you said you wanted to no about our going to
taladega to drill I have not herd nothing about it since we got down
here only our colonel says that we may have our first battle here at this
place I expect we will stay here a good while and we may never leave
here while the war lasts we have not drilled any yet but the captain
says we will have to go at it the 10 of this month he thinks that we
will draw our saddles the ninth my horse is very bad off with the dis-
temper he has eat nothing hardly for about a week ould Deny kelly is
down here and he brought us a backet full of eggs which we was very
glad to receive you said you wanted to no what to do with them stands
tell manuel to put them in the stillhouse on the flore if robberson dont
come and do that work dont pay him for it nothing more at present
for I cant think of half that I want to rite give my love to lis and that
I would bee glad to see her I would bee glad to see little ginny[12] and
give her a kiss and see the rest of the children frolic around and play
on my lap and see babe suck his thum if it had not have bee the love
I have for them and my country I would have been ther now nothing
more but remain you affectionate husband til death J W Cotton to
Mariah Cotton there is about fore thousand soldiers stationed here
now and there is more comeing in direct your letters to John W. Cotton Montgomery Alabama in care of Capt M G Slaughter

May the 6 1862
nothing more had happened since yesterday we went on dress perraid
yesterday and to day we have not put out no gards around the encamp-
ment yet we are doing nothing yet but go to town or anywhere else we

---

[11] The Alabama River flows by Montgomery.

[12] "Little Ginny" was the baby when Cotton went to war. She seems to have
been a delicate child and her father was constantly worried about her health. When
she was "fat and sassa" he was happy indeed. She grew to maturity in spite of his
fears, married John C. Monk, who lived just down the road, and reared a family.
Mrs. Arah P. Stanley, who now owns the letters, is her granddaughter.

want to I dont mind any thing that is to do here only having to stay
from home I am well today but some of the company is complaining
I have just now received a letter from you and I was glad to here from
you and to here that you all was well and that all was going on well
and that the wheat was doing better I want to see you and the children as bad as any body can

Alabama Coosa County[13] June the 7 1862
Mariah Cotton   Dear wife I take my pen in hand to rite you a few
lines to let you no that I am well and I hope these few lines may find
you an the children all well dock has been very sick but he is a good
deal better he had like to have dide nite before last he had the con-
gestive fever in his head he left here this morning on the cars to go to
georgia on a 14 day furlow[14] the rest of us are well except william lessley he is complaining some the most of our men has gone home with
the measles we are not doing any thing here only lying about I reckon
you found that I did not come home when the captain comes home I
will try to come home he will bee back next wednesday if I dont get
to come back home you must do the best you can have that wheat and
barley thrashed as soon as you can and turn the hogs in and dont let
pares[15] nor ases[16] in and have the ry cut and thrashed[17] the yankeys

[13] This must be a slip of the pen for the letter indicates he was still near Montgomery.
[14] Dr. Hindsman seemed to have shuttled between Coweta County and Coosa
County. In 1861, he was practicing medicine near Grantville, Georgia, but he enlisted from Coosa County in 1862. His wife was in Georgia part of the time and
either with or near Mrs. Cotton the other. After the war apparently Dr. Hindsman
settled in Coosa County, although no evidence has yet turned up that he was practicing medicine. (Mary G. Jones and Lily Reynolds, *Coweta County Chronicles for
One Hundred Years with an account of the Indians from Whom Land was Acquired
and Some Historical Papers Relating to its Acquisition by Georgia with Lineage
Pages*, Atlanta, Georgia, Steen Printing Co., 1928. Page 145. *Muster Roll*). He
with Mariah Cotton was one of the administrators of the estate of John W. Cotton.
(*Minutes of the Probate Court*, Coosa County) IX, 669. Later he moved to Dallas,
Texas, and "made his fortune" in his profession (Mrs. Jefferson Davis Cotton to
Lucille Griffith, June 10, 1950.)
[15] "Par" is his father, Cary Cotton, a man of some substance. He owned (1860)
150 acres of improved land, 690 acres of unimproved, all valued at $5,500. Among
the livestock were 100 hogs (*Eighth Census*, Schedule 4, Production of Agriculture
in the 2nd Subdivision in the County of Coosa, Mt. Olive, p. 13). Mrs. Cotton's
father is "pap".
[16] Asa Waldrop, a near neighbor, was a brother-in-law. His wife was Nancy
Cotton, a sister of John W. Cotton. The house in which they lived is still standing
near the Mt. Pleasant Church cemetery in Coosa County. Both Waldrops are buried in Mt. Pleasant cemetery as are the Cottons and many of their relatives.
[17] The Cottons were general farmers and Mr. Cotton was especially interested in

are all gone from here but some sick ones I believe that every thing is till riseing here I had to pay fifty cent a quire for this paper I have nothing of importance to rite there has been a big battle at richmon[18] but no correct account how many were killed on neither side nothing more at present but remain your affectionate husband til death

John W Cotton

Montgomery Alabama June the 17 1862 Dear wife I again address you with a few lines to let you no that I am well and hope these few lines may find you and the children all well I have not much to rite I hant herd from dock since monday I got a letter from lis she said that he was very porely our captain came home yesterday and several others and we went on drill this morning for the first time since I have been down here he says tomorrow that he will drill all that hant got saddles on foot we have not drown no saddles yet I dont no whether I shal get to come home any more before we leave here or not they say that the colonel has stopped giving furlos to any body a good many thinks we will leave here in a short time and go to chatanuga georgia if we stay here I want frar or wash[19] or Bill to come down here and bring us some vegetables for they are very hy here I baught some irish potatoes this morning at 15cts a quart if they do come and you have more bacon than you need get them to bring it and sell it it is worth forty cts a pound and from that to fifty I went to meetin las sunday and I herd the romon catholieks and presbyterians[20] both preach and we had meeting at our camp that nite and again last nite the regiment that was here when we came here is ordered off to florida there is now twenty eight or twenty nine companys in the legion nothing more at present I remain your affectionate husband til death

John W Cotton

rite I hanent got nary letter from you yet

---

the grains. Note his frequent mention of the wheat. In addition to the crops here named, the farm produced livestock, corn, oats, peas and sweet potatoes in quantities large enough to be included in the census (*Eighth Census,* Agriculture, Coosa County, Schedule 4, p. 138).

18 The Peninsular campaign under General George McClellan.

19 Probably Wash Smith, the husband of Cotton's sister Mary Ann.

20 There is nothing in the letters to indicate the denomination of the Cottons but they were Primitive Baptists (Mrs. Arah P. Stanley). Mt. Pleasant Baptist Church was Primitive.

Montgomery June the 19. 1862

Dear wife I seat my self to rite you a few lines to let you no that I received a letter from you las eavning and was glad to here from you all but I was sorry to here that little ginny was sick I hope that she is better by this time if any of you gets sick and you think you need a doctor it is not so fare to bakers but what you can send for him if you need any abit medicine send to william words and you can get plenty he lives one mild this side of bill adkinses these lines leave me well and all of our boys but there is some of our company complaining and a great many at home sick I hant herd from dock since last monday was a weak ago I dont no why he dont rite and let us no how he is   it was thought last weak that we would have been gone from here before now but the legion is now turned into a brigade and it will take some time fifteen or twenty days to get ready to leave here I am going to try to come home before we leave here if I can the colonel says there shall bee no more furlows given to well men but some of the captains gaves furlows any how everything is still riseing yet bacon is worth from 40 to 50 cts per pound flour 9 cts per pound butter forty cts per pound cabbage twenty five cts a head irish potatoes 20 cts a quart and beens the same and everything else according I want you to rite and let me no how you all getting long I want to here from little ginney again very bad I shall bee uneasy until I here from her again nothing more at present but remain your affectionate husband til death John W Cotton

Montgomery Alabama June the 23 1862

Mariah Cotton Dear wife I take my pen in hand to rite you a few lines to let you no that I am well and hope these lines may find you all well but I am a fraid that little ginney has not got well I want to here from her very bad I have not received but one letter from you since I left home I tryed to come home to see little ginney but I couldnot get off the legion will bee formed in to battalions this weak and the offecers elected[21] hant mutch to rite I got a letter from dock day before yesterday he is very porley yet he said he had one of his bad spells yesterday was a weak ago that lasted him for 10 hours the boys here are well but william lessley he is complaining rite smart ly and one with the measles he is the last one in the company to have them

---

[21] In the act that provided for bounties section 4 provided that troops elect company officers (*Statutes*, I, 223. December 11, 1861).

the Colonel says that we will get our equipment soon bill[22] is getting
fat again he is most well of the dis temper our horses are all doing well
rite when you can and tell me how things are going on nothing more
at present but remain your affectionate husband til death John W
Cotton

Georgia Coweta County   July the 10. 1862
dear wife   I now seat myself to rite you a few lines to let you no that
I am at John Fulmers[23] and I am well all of them here is well your
paps folks are all well but mike[24] and he is able to rock about he is at
home on 30 days furlough and so is John Tramel[25] me and dock left
montgomery yesterday morning and we staid at your paps last nite our
company was to leave to day and we are to meat it tomorrow at grants-
ville and go on with them we are going to atlanta I would bee very
glad to here from you all for I hant herd from you since I left home[26]
I want you to rite to me as soon as you get this letter direct your letter
to Atlanta georgia I am getting very anxious to here from you all let
me no how manuel comes on with his crop and every thing and how
the hogs are doing we have drawn our sabers and haver sacks but the
rest of our arms and our canteens we aim to get at atlanta and our
uniforms our saddles are makeing at augusta we will get them in a
weak or two crops looke only tolerable well there ant mutch cotton
planted out here your pap and all of them was very glad to see me but
none of them wernt looking for me I hant mutch to rite to you nothing more at present but remain your affectionate husband til death
                                   John W Cotton

22 "Bill" here is his horse but the reader has to learn it from the context.   The
same name may be a neighbor.
23 The Reverend John W. Fulmer (1825-1903), a Baptist minister, was the husband of Rachel Cotton, another sister of John W. Cotton.   They later moved to
Coosa County and are buried in the Mt. Pleasant cemetery along with the Cottons.
It was a Primitive Baptist Church (the building has been razed but the site is
plainly visible and the cemetery is still there), on the road between Hanover and
Mt. Olive. Mr. Fulmer, although he was buried there, probably was not of the
Primitive Church for he was pastor of the Mt. Olive Church (Missionary Baptist)
for thirty-five years.   (George E. Brewer, "History of Coosa County", *Alabama
Historical Quarterly*, Summer issue, 1942, p. 164).   Mrs. Jefferson Davis Cotton,
daughter-in-law of John W. Cotton is still living in Coweta County, Georgia, and
she says this is true.
24 Michael Hindsman, a brother of Mrs. Cotton.
25 John Trammell was the husband of Mrs. Cotton's sister Nancy.
26 Cotton's furloughs are hard to determine but since he had already acknowl-
edged several letters from his wife, he must have been home between June 23, and
July 10.

July 11 we are at grantville waiting for the cars and our company but we dont no whether they will come up or not if they dont come up they will rite to us they may have past last nite but no body cant tell here the car last nite never stoped these lines leave me well nothing more

Atlanta Georgia July 13th 1862
Mariah dear wife I again take my pen in hand to drop you a few lines to let you no where I am and that I am well and I hope these few lines may find you all enjoying the same blessing I want to here from you very bad worse than I ever did in my life but I am afraid it will bee some time before I can here from you we got moved out of town yesterday and got our tents put up and every thing fited for staying here and this morning we received orders to move from here we are camped about two miles above atlanta we have got good water here and a helthy looking place we are camped in three hundred yars of that great steem distillery you have herd talk of but they are not stilling now I hant mutch to rite only to you only to let you no where I am Aasa went down to his fathers yesterday eaving to come back tuesday and he dont no that we are ordered off from here I want you to rite to me as soon as you get these direct your letter to Chatanuga tennessee in care of Captain M. G. Slaughter hilliards legion I reckon that we will stay there til we get equiped and armed they are expecting to have a fight there before long they have just now come here with the drays after our baggage to carry it to the cars to be ready to start in the morning I dont want you to uneasy yourself about me for I am doing very well bill is complaining right smart the rest of our boys is well nothing now but remain your affectionate husband til death
John W Cotton

Now in a fare land I rome
fare from my friend at home
but I hope the time is near
when we shall all meet again
I have not herd from home since
I left there.[27]

---

[27] These attempts at homemade verse are interesting. Some of the "poetry" was current among soldiers; some obviously composed at the moment. Compare with verse of January 19, 1863. Even Mrs. Cotton tried her hand at it, July 19, 1863, but the "song ballet" is missing. Bell Irvin Wiley in *Life of Johnny Reb*, New York: Bobbs-Merrill (1943) has a good chapter on this subject.

Chattanooga Tennessee July the 16 1862

Dear wife I now once more take my pen in hand to rite you a few
more lines to let you no where I am and how I am I am as well as I
ever was in my life and I hope these few lines may reach you all the
same I got the letter that you sent to me by James Arnold I saw him
at dalton in georgia him and frank Corley stopped there weighting
for passage on the cars and we over took them and they went to noxville and we went to chattanooga I was very glad to here from you it
was the first time since I left home I would bee glad to here from you
all again today I rote to you last sunday when we were at atlanta we
left there monday morning at ten oclock and we landed at Chattanooga at twelve oclock that night we had a very pleasant trip of it but
our horses saw sights they had to do about twenty five hours without
any thing to eat and some of the lasy never even watered there horses
when we got here that nite some of them never wated to attend to
any thing and others watered there horses and we never got them of on
the cars til 8 or 9 oclock next morning we got nearly all of our things
halled out to the camp yesterday we are camped five miles from Chattanooga we have a very rough place here it is rite in the woods on the
foot of a mountain they say the yankeys are in about fifteen miles of
here but the main armey is about thirty miles of here on the tennessee
river it is clost to us about a half mild we have got nearly all of our
company to gether now we left our first lieutenant[28] at montgomery
and it is thought he will die he has got the brain fever there is about
forty thousand of our troops here and about forty thousand yankeys
but our men dont appear to fer them no more than if they wernt here
there is strong talk of us beeing dismounted if we are there will bee a
set of mad men for aheap of them says they are not able to stand the
infantry I had rather not bee dismounted they say they will pay us for
our horses but we are not willing to sell them the boys the most of
them are very mutch dissatisfyed here they want to go back some where
when we came up the people cheerd us all the way men women and
children they were collected on the road in great quantities and there
was a continuel hollow nearly all the way we passed some of the higest
bridgs that ever I saw and we passed the tunnel under the stone mountain but it was night and we couldnot see mutch when we struck it I
could not harly here any thing for the shouts of the boy nothing more
at present but remain your affectionate friend til death   John W. Cotton

28 William W. Lee (*Muster Roll*) .

rite to me and direct your letter to John W. Cotton Chattanooga Tennessee in care of M. G. Slaughter Hilliards legion when this you see remember me

Chattanooga Tennessee July the 21 1862
Mariah Dear wife I once more take the pleasure to rite you a few lines to let you no that I am well but dock is sick he has had one of his bad spells it was the worst he ever had but he is better he is able to set up a rite smart the rest of our boys are tolerable well but several of our company is sick more with the yellow janders[29] than anything else I hope these few lines may find you all well and I hope that you have become reconciled about my beeing from home for there is no chance now for me to come to see you all there is no chance to get a furlow sick or well unless they think we are going to dye I want to here from you very bad for I havent herd from you since I saw James arnold I have rote you three letters one at John Fulmers and one at atlanta and one since I come here and I hant got nary answer yet if you hant rote rite when you get this letter I hant mutch to rite to you we are doing nothing yet we hant got our saddles yet nor nothing else but some ould sabers and haver sacks mussels to feed our horses in and I dont no when we will get any thing else we get a plenty to eat and a plenty to give our horses I expect you here a great deal about a fight at this place but there is no danger here of a fight at present I dont think they have armed all of the legion but our battalion there is a great many soldiers around here I saw hiram smith and lige gaden yesterday in a texes regiment they are camped about a haf a mild from us I herd about uncle micane Cotton and where he lives and they told me about all of the georgia boys they say uncla weave[30] is doing mity well now he is raising stock and has got a very good wife they say Jack welch is doing very well but John is not doing as well and Jim weaks is doing very well uncle weave lives in Houghman county Houghman post office If I could see you now I could tell you a great deal that I cant rite have all of your peeches stilled[31] that you can I was sorry that I did

29 Yellow jaundice.
30 Weaver, Cary and Eli Cotton were among the early settlers around Grantville, Georgia. Mary G. Jones and Lily Reynolds, *Coweta County Chronicles for One Hundred Years with an Account and Some Historical Papers Relating to its Acquisition By Georgia with Lineage Papers,* Atlanta, Steen Printing Co., 1928, p. 811. (Cited hereafter as *Chronicles*).
31 This the first of several references to the "peech" and other fruit brandy. Fruit was abundant and brandy brought a good price. Repeatedly he advised his wife to "hold onto" the brandy for she would be able to get anything she asked

not get them apples you sent to me by Jim Arnol when you rite to me
rite how your crop is comeing on and what manuel is getting on nothing more at present only remain your most affectionate husband til
death John W Cotton to his wife at home when this you see remember
me and I will never for get the

Chattanooga tennessee July the 28th 1862
My dear wife and family I once more hasten to rite you a few lines
to let you no I am well I have had the roseola but I am well now I
hope these few lines may find you all well and enjoying the same
blessing I have not received nary letter from you since James Arnold
brought me that one I never wanted to here from home any worse
then I do now I think certainly you have rote but I have not received
your letters this is fore since we got to Chattanooga I am now in the
horsepitol waiting on the sick our captain sent ten men to the horsepitol yesterday and sent me to wait on them dock was one of them he
has had one of his bad spells but is a grat deal better he can walk over
the house a little there is about 25 of our men on the sick list we have
moved from where we were nerer town to camp shorter[32] we have a
very comfortable horsepital and it is kept very nice and the soldiers is
treated very well I dont no how long I will stay here I get $7.50cts[33]
more for staying here than I were getting but there is a great deal to
do here we have from 8 to 10 men to nurse a pease I want you to
rite I want to here from you very bad and no how things is going on
and how the children is getting on with the measles. there is a big
fight expected here or here about not fur off soldiers are landing here
by thousands I am setting in a window riting where I can see all over
Chattanooga it is a sonny looking place rite in a hollow between two
mountains and on the tennessee river it is about the sise of wetumpka
this is a heap mor broken a place than coosa county we are at the foot
of look out mountain william lessley has got the yellow ganders but is
better of them Aasa is well I hant got time to rite very much but if I
could see you I could tell you a great deal that I cant rite asa rote nan
a letter yesterday and I rote lis a letter today for dock I [?] thursday
for your pap to come after dock I think he will get a discharge he has

---

for it. The area seems to be favorable to fruit even yet. In April, 1950, when this
writer visited the Cotton house site, there was blooming a stub of a peach tree,
a carpet of wild strawberries, blackberries by the acres and a lot of wild plums.

[32] Many of the camps have names by courtesy only for often they were nothing
except a temporary stopping place.

[33] His basic pay in the cavalry was $12.00 per month.

got to the place he cant hardly here atall but he may soon get over that I want you to write as soon as you get this letter for you dont no how bad I want to here from you nothing more at present I remain your most affectionate husband til death John W Cotton
Direct your letters to John W Cotton
Chattanooga Tennessee in care of Captain M. G. Slaughter hilliards Legion Cavalry battallion

Chattanooga Tennessee August 1th 1862
Great god what a thunder bolt struck my ear yesterday when Asa come up here to the horsepitle and gave me a letter from you and told me that Cricket[34] was dead I no not how to address you on the subjectt I hop she is better off but it almost brakes my hart to think I could not bee at home and see the last of her I want you to grieve as little as possible I hope the time is near at hand when I can come home and stay with you and the rest of the children I hope these few lines may find you all well I am not very well at this time I have sit up of nites and waited on the sick til I am wore out and grived to death I am not sick only from grief I dont aim to stay here much longer our company is ordered off from here to louden tennessee they are sending up all of the sick from here that is able to go there is a big battle expected here soon and I want to see it come on I had rather dy than live if it want for you sake and the children I want to see you worse than I ever did in my life and talk with you I dont no what to rite to you I want you to rite me a letter of consolation as soon as you get this letter dock is better all but his head he cant here any yet lis is here she is trying to get a discharge for dock and I think she will get it for him she was here when I got your letter I reckon they will leave to morrow and I will go back to camps I dont no when we will leave here if ther is a fite here we wont have no hand in it we hant got our equipage yet the captain is gone after our saddles now you need not bee uneasy about me if I get killed just say I dyed in a good cause ould abe lincon and his cabinet could not daunt me now I could fall his hole army rite now I dont feel like riting now but I will try to rite you another letter in a few days forgive me for not riting no more if I could see you I could talk to you a weak but I cant rite what I could tell you if I

---

[34] Nancy Hanner, born February 3, 1858. She had died July 12, twelve days before this letter was written (family Bible). This is one of the most touching letters he wrote his wife. Read also the ones from Mrs. Cotton to her husband about the child's death dated August 21 and 25.

could see you nothing more at present only I remain your affectionate
husband til death John W. Cotton

                    Chattanooga Tennessee   August the 3 1862
My dar wife and children   I now with mutch sorrow attempt to rite
you a few more lines to let you no that I am not very well I have got
a bad cold but not very bad off I left the horsepitol yesterday eavning
they have sent docks to atlanta and all of the rest that was able to go
I hope him and his on the cars to start   I never want to go to a horse
pital again men are dying there constant there was about a dozen men
dyed while I was there three of our own men and we have two more
that I think well dye and lots more sick but I dont no how many asa
is not very well he says he thinks he is takeing the yellow janders william lessley has got well the helth of our company is very bad we are
now ordered from here to louden tennessee we will leave here in the
morning and we hant got our saddles nor arms yet all of the other
companys in the batalion has got saddles but ourn and I reckon they
will lend us saddles to ride it is eighty miles from here and we have
got to go by land Phelit and John Sarel is at home sick lis did not get
dock no discharge tell nan I was glad to get her kind and consoleing
letter tell her I cant rite to her now I hant got time for it is getting
late in the eavning I dont want you to grieve two mutch about the
death of our lettle daughter we must only hope that she is better off
than we are but oh how I will miss her when I come home she will
not be there to fondle on my nees with the rest of the children   I hope
the rest may do well til I come home and want you to take care of
yourself and not expose your self two mutch nan rote that bill had
gone after cousin carline walker to come and stay with you if she has
come tell her to take good care of you and the children til I come home
nan said that letha had been staying with you   tell her I am more than
a thousand times oblige to her for her kindness towards you for I no
you needed somebody to stay with you I hant mutch to rite to console
you for I am in two mutch trouble myself I shall bee uneasy til I here
that all of the children has had the measles and well of them   I never
new what pleasure home afforded to a man before If it were not for
the love of my country and family and the patriotism that bury in my
bosom for them I would bee glad to come home and stay there but I
no I have as much to fite for as any body else but if I were there I no
I could not stay so I have to take it as easy as possible let nan reed this
letter nan rite to me when you can asa rote to you today   Mariah rite

when you can I hav not got but the two letters since I left home I would love to here from you every day I rote you one day before yesterday excuse my bad riting and spelling for I am riting on my nee siting on a log nothing more at present I remain your most affectionate husband and friend til death John W. Cotton to his wife at home.

Alexandres Hospital Atlanta Ga August 15/62
Mrs. Cotton Dear Madam[35]

I take pleasure in writing you few lines for Mr. Cotton or rather his request to inform you that he is not improving very much yet Dr giving him quinine very heavey today which makes his head in an aw-full fire his fever has never broke yet the Dr has never given hem any strong medisin until today since he has been here he came here last Thursday evening which was the 14th of the month I think he looks better today then he did yesterday I think he will be up in a few days he said for you to write to him soon as you get this let him know how you all are getting on how your crops is Mrs Cotton I will keep you posted how Mr Cotton get on as long as I stay here but I may have to leave for my company this week we both belong to the same company we are not in the same Hospital though I can go and see him every day write to him Atlanta Ga Alexander Hospital as for the health of our company I cant tell anything about for I have not been with the Company 3 weeks or more I learn that they are at or above Knoxville tenne Nothing more at present will write again in a few days to you believe me to be your friend & your trula
To Mrs Cotton

W. G. Johnson
John W Cotton

Atlanta August 17, 1862
Mariah dear wife I now attemp to let you no that am in the All-Scrandrer horsepitle I am god deale better than I was when I come heare the Dr Says I have got the typhoid fevor but he says he will have me up in afew days I come hear the 14th of this month I cant write much as I am Sick and Nurvess I had to git the nurs to do my writeing I hope I will be able to giv you afull histor of all things i afew days I want you to write to me as soon as you git this letter direct your letter

---

[35] This letter of course was not written by John W. Cotton but there is no fur-ther knowledge as to who the scribe is. As is revealed in the next letter Cotton had typhoid fever and his low spirits evidenced in earlier letters may be in part explained by this illness.

to Allesander atlanta ga Hospitle atlanta ga I clos my letter by Singing my Name John W. Cotton

Atlanta Georgia Alexandres horsepital August the 25, 1862
Dear wife I take my pen in hand to let you no now I am getting along I am still on the mend but I gain strength very slow I   long enough to rite but a few lines at a time I am not in any misery at all I can get up and walk across my room and back to my bad I was taken sick at the horsepital waiting on bud I went back to my company on saturday and that nite I tuck a dose of pills that   and on monday morning we tuck up the line of march to louden but when we got there we never stopped we went on to noxville and I kept getting worse all of the way I gave out 23 miles this side of noxville and they put me on the cars and sent me to noxville to the horsepitol James dukes says I stayed there 4½ days I dont reccollect how long for every thing seams like a dream while I was there they put me on the cars one nite a little after dark to come to Atlanta we got there the next morning every thing seams like a dream til I had been here two or three days I xpect it will bee a long time before I am able to leave here rite as soon as your get this letter and let me no how things are going on when manuel gets redy to split rails tell him to split rails on the ridg from the horse lot over towards where we drug them ded horses and if there ant timber enough there cut all of the ded timber from the cowpen to the tip of the hill towards moses nothing more at present but remain your affectionate husband til death   John W Cotton

Alabama   Coosa Count   August the 21 1862
   my dear husband I now seat my self to rite you a few to let you hear from me and the children the children is all at well at time and as for my self I am not atall sick but I trouble all most to death about you and our little cricket death it all most breaks my hart to think that you are gone so farr off from me and the children but I can ony hope that the time is coming when you will get home to us all again I hope thes few lines many find you well evreything is doing very well you stock is all doing vary well so far   I hant much of importen to rite to you for I cant hear of eny thing hear but war all the time   they say tha are fixing for a big battle at richmond[36] again   I want you to rite to me weth you gon fether of than you wer before or not and rite

---

[36] Actually there was little fighting very near Richmond but several battles were fought in the area in the Second Bull Run Campaign, August 23-September 1.

to me all about how you far wether you get annuf to eat or not   I hear
of som not getting anuf to eat   I so uneasy about you not geting anuf
to eat so I want to no you par is still yet he get a heep of peches and
appels   Mr. Norwood com and tuck up his nodt that I had wash com
with him you undel John Tate was out hear a while back he sed tha
had had no rain in about twelve weeks he sed tha was bount up he
sed he wood bee back hear in about too weeks he sed that he was com
to fech his wool he sed that we all mite have some wool it is seling at
a dollar per pount you par sed he think that I will make a mity good
crop of corne ther is a heep of complant about sarrow crop I dont no
what will become of us all crop is sarrow and worms is eaten up the
grass and ther is som on the fodder I dont no whether tha will hurt
the fodder or not you brouther William and the rest of the conscript
men started from around hear the 19 of this[37] thear is a tauke of thear
taken of than hier than thirty five but I hope that wont take no more
I wont than that is thear to com home   wever do you want me to sell
any of you weet for seed or not you rite to me about what to do about
it you must rite me all the good advice you can for I need advice you
no I receive a letter from you a Monday it is now thursday it was date
the third of this I was glad to fom you I was sorrow to hear that you
and asa was not well I so uneasy about you I dont what to do I wood
this hold world if you was at home with me so I cood no when you
sick or well you sed that you wood bee uneasy till you heard that the
children was all well of the measels tha are all well of them now sweet
and Jinny has no had than yet   I dont think tha will have them now
so you must not uneasy you self about the measells now sinch I cem-
mence this letter nancy com up hear with a letter that she got today
from asa it was date 11 and it sed that you was in the horsepitol sick
you dont no how bad I felt to hear of you beeing in a horsepitol sick
Oh that I ony cood bee ther to wate on you   I will bee so uneasy till
hear from you I cant rest but I hope you are better by this time and I
hope by the time you get this letter you will bee well   Mr. Lessley got a
letter William Lessley that was date the 19 it sed you was sick he sed
tha had sent the sick to Atlanta and so I dont no wat to do about sending this letter and so I did not send it I nevery was as uneasy in my life
nuth mor at present but remain you affecttion wife until death Mariah
Cotton[38]

---

[37] The conscript law, drafting men between 18 and 35, had passed April 16,
1862 (*Statutes*, II, 29-32).

[38] Mrs. Cotton's spelling, handwriting and composition indicate she had less

(Post script to letter begun August 21 1862)
You brouth Willan sed he want to see you while he is at home a ferlow
he sed you must get well as soon as you can and com hear home charo-
line sed you rote to her to take ker of me and children sed she will do
that the best she can she sed you no how bad she want you well and
com home ann sed she want see you mity bad this a peece that charo-
line and William and ann rote you tha are willing for me to come to
see you

August the 25 1862

my dear husband   I wonce more with sorrow and trouble I take my
pen in hand to rite you a few lines to let you hear from me and the
children the children is all well at this time I am well all to grief and
sarrow   I have gest now receive a letter from you it give me relief for
I did not no wher you was I never was as glad to hear fom any boddy
in my life as I was to hear from you I am so sarrow to hear of you
beein sick I dont no how to address you on it I dont want you to bee
uneasy about home I wont you to take good cear of you self and try
to get well again I want to come and see you if you are willing and are
a gouing to stay ther long anuft for me to com and if you are rite me
about it whether I must try to come or nor   if you are abl to write
and if I cood see you I cood tell you aheap I nevr wanted to see any
boddy as bad in my life as I want to see you now and wate on you   if
you are willing for me to try to come to see you you must rite soon I
had a letter rote to send to you but I heard that you was sent to atlanta and I kept it I did not have the paper all full and I thought I
wood rite this letter on it and send it all to you you must excuse my
bad spelling and riten for it is hard task for me to rite to you now I
wish I cood hear from you every our rite to me if you dont want some
clouse while you are ther and if you do rite what it is and I will try
to send it or fetch it I wood bee son glad if you cood come home and
stay till you got well this is the first chanch I had to send of a letter
sench I got you our male is not regular yet it is to start this weaker tha
say you must rite when you can if you are able to rite I wich I could
get a letter from you evry day I hant hourd a word from bud and lis
sench you rote I rote to you was gon but he come back yesterday on a
furlow if ther is any chance for you to com home till you get well I

education than her husband. It is possible that this letter was never mailed to her
husband and therefore was saved with his. In the Coweta County, Georgia, records
several members of her family sign with a mark.

want to no it Nan sed she will stay with sharotine and the children
till I can com to see you I will close my few remarks to you rite soon
Mariah Cotton to her loving husband John W. Cotton

Ala Coosa Co Septemver the 9 1862
Dear brother and sister I take this opportunity to rite you a few lines
to let you no that we are all well and have been every sence mariah has
been gone only sweet eat too many beens and made him sick a day
and nite I hope these few lines may find you all well I have been waiting and looking for a letter from you but I have concluded to rite
any how and not wait no longer mariah promised to rite to me about
making clothes I have got the [   ]³⁹ of some wooll Asa rote to me
to make him a coat and vest and pants and a blanket as soon and he
said to make the tails of his coat long and the waist of his pants longer
I have spoak to Miss Corley for her [   ]³⁹ she is making provided I
cant get wool enough asa rote to me that his pants is a geting thin I
want you to rite to me as soon as you get this letter and tell me how
long you think you will stay there and if you cant take asa some
clothes that we have got maid when pa comes after mariah he talks
about going to wilks when he comes there to see about that property
we have made tow shirts I would be very glad if you could take what
clothes we have got made for fear when we undertake to send them
that you will never get them I dont no when asa aims to come there
he has got some fruit to still next monday he is done all to that but I
dont no what he will do about comeing I have come to pars since I
commenced my letter he sas he hant a going to wilks if I can get him to
cary the things to newan and put them on the cars I will send them to
you if you say you want them and can carry them clothese to asa   lily
and caroline was married sonday morning I do not no what he aims to
do though I think he aims to live here there to live with mariah like
she has been a hiring manyel is a getting too big for his breeches he
went off saturday at dinner and never come home tell monday about
nine oclock and left 2 or 3 days pulling of fodder down and the most of
it cured and when he come home I said something to him and he got
so mad he jawed me to the[   ]³⁹ he is a going to take five days
hollyday let mariah say what she will he sais it was nothing but contry
that mariah did not hire some body to help him pull fodder⁴⁰ tell all
the connection howda for me give my love to all the pople ther in my

---

³⁹ Torn manuscript.
⁴⁰ This is the only record of trouble with Manuel. See letter of September 7.

old Settlement I would come out to see them when pa comes if I had a way to get back tell John Fulmer to move out here Nancy Waldrop to mariah Cotton and John W. Cotton Weaver rite to me how many oats you want me to save for you so many people is a wanting oats brownt folks has got the dipthera and i am afraid we will al get it for manueal goes to browns[41] so much pa would whipped him yesterday but he had a sore finger

Atlanta Georgia September the 12. 1862 Mariah Dear wife I received your letter this morning and was very glad to here from you and that you was well but very sorry to here that little ginney wer so sick I was in hopes that she had got well but I new that there were something the matter that you did not come back but I never thought of the small pox stopping you I was so uneasy I did not no what to do til I got your letter I was a fraid you was sick I am a fraid you wont get to come atall I shall bee very sorry if you dont get to come for I had a great del to tell you when par comes tell him to come and see me if he can I hant herd from home since you left here I am still mending I have got so I can walk about a rite smart by takeing my time I went to the car shed last night and nite before to meet you but I never found you nor ginny I think I will go again to nite and look for you our sick men are all mending at present that man in our room that had the phneumonier is dead there is a talk here about breaking up all of the horsepitals and send all that is ablt to go home and them that is not able keep them til they git able they have turned out all of them prisoners they had in the gard house when you was here I want you to rite as soon as you git this letter and let me no how you all are and if the small pox is spreading any and I want you to rite the day before you start home   if you dont get to come to see me no more nothing more at present but remain you affectionate friend til death

John W. Cotton

Atlanta Georgia   september the 15 1862
dear wife it is with mutch grief and fear that I take my pen in hand to let you no that I red your kind letter this morning and was glad to here from you again but was very sorry to here that little ginney was so sick I was in hopes that when I herd from her again she would bee well but I am glad to think that she is better or that you think so I have received both of your letters and was ectremely glad to here from you for I have been uneasy ever since you left here about little ginney

[41] This is probably the Brown family that owned Manuel.

I am very sorry that you could not come back to see me but I am in hopes now that I will get to come to see you they say the horsepitals will be broke up in a day or two and all that ant able to go to there companys and are able to go home will be furlowed home til they get well and them that are not able to go home will stay here til they get able to go home if I get a furlow you ant to see me coming down on the first train I am still mending some I am a great deal better off than I was when you left me I have got so I can eat a plenty I bought me some potatoes this morning and are having me a rich pie made for dinner I have eat up my ham and drunk up my brandy and want more if I dont get a furlow I would bee very glad for par to come to see me when he comes out after you tell him to come if he can the [?] told some men that is going to there companys that this horsepital could brake up tomorrow they are building houses out at the fareground to put the sick in and they are moveing bunks out there now you need not look for for I dont no whether I will get to come or not but I hope I will that would cure my uneasiness I got a letter from nan this morning which hepe my feeling some I will send it to you I got a letter from Asa dated the 10 he said he and porter was well except bad cold our company was then at nacville and he said he did not no when they would leave there he said they mite leave in a day or two and they mite stay there a good while he said my horse was fatning eye will not rite any thing to you now about affairs at home now from what I can lern if is not worth while to make me any close for if I go to my company before I get them I will never get them if I had what close I have got at home they would do me very well and you had better send them to me if you get home time enough by express nothing more at present but remain you best friend and affectionate husband til death John W. Cotton   I hope little ginny will get well but I fear

Atlanta ga September the 17 1862   Dear wife it is with much uneasiness I attempt to rite you a few lines to let you no that I am still mending I am getting along very well considering I am in sow much trouble I would gave any thing to see you and little ginney I hope these few lines may find you well and little ginney better and all of the connection well I looked for a letter from you yesterday or this morning but did not get it I want you to rite to me at least every other day til you go home[42] I dont expect par will come as soon as you looked for him from what nans letter said about it   I dont expect wash got

42 Mrs. Cotton was at the home of her father near Grantville, Georgia. The homestead is near the highway between Newnan and LaGrange and is closer to

the letter I rote him nor nan never got hern nor you never got the
first one I rote to you I have got two from you since you left here I am
very sorry that you could not come back to see me yet we must take
things as they come and greeve as little as possible maby the war wont
last always and we will bee free again to enjoy our freedom at home as
we see proper you need not hurry home to make me any close for from
what I can lern I never could get them after I leave here Nan spoke of
sending me and Asa some close by par if she dont we will have to de-
pend on the yankeys for them I am afraid you cant get home time enough to send me any or I would want you to send me some by express
you could send them to montgomery and then there by express I expect
they will want to send me off before long if I keep mending our horsepitol has not broke up yet nor I dont no exactly when it will they
have discharged several last nite and this morning and are sending off
all that are able to go   I think they are waiting for further orders
from the war department if I could get to go home I could make all
necessary arrangements about clothing but that is uncertain if they
broke up the horsepitols about my getting a furlow when you go home
I want you to send for par ever time manuel crooks his finger til he
gets him straight tell par if there is any work he wants to swop I want
him to do it so he can help him under charge I recken he will swop
in gatherin corn I want the fresh field all sowed in wheat if the fresh
part is not two fowl what lay out must bee broke up first then sowed I
want the oald field on the creek sowed in rye what lay out rite off as
soon as possible and the peech orcherd in rye romane[43] at present John
W. Cotton

September
the 25-1862

Atlanta Ga. Medical College Horsepital Mariah Cotton Dear wife I
once more take my pen in hand to drop you a few lines to let you
no that I am well and still mending I hope these few lines may find
you and all of the children enjoying the same blessing I hope that
little ginney is getting well as fast as she can and eye hope that babies

---

Moreland than Grantville. Her father was William Hindsman who was married to
Nancy Cotton, sister of Cary Cotton, making Mariah Hindsman Cotton a first
cousin to her husband. (Mrs. Jefferson Davis Cotton to Lucille Griffith, June 10,
1950; Settlement of Life Estate, *Deed Book,* [Coweta County, Georgia] p. 72; Court
of Ordinary [Coweta County] *Return Book,* Book R, p. 700-703).

43 One of the values of these letters is that they give an insight into small farming. Some time the advice is specific as it is here and at other times it is general.
"Do the best you know how" is a frequent refrain.

getting fat and all of the rest doeing well and I hope all of the connection is well I got a letter last nite from Alben Martin from knoxville which I will send to you he says my company left knoxville the
18 of this month he said that all of the company wus well but dock he
said he had the neuralga in his jaw and the thotache but you can reed
for your self and see what he says I bought me a very good wescoat for
two dollars but I think I cheated the fellow he threw down a hole pile
of oald corse thing on the counter and told me to pick out one for
two dollars and there was one good one in the pile and I put it on
and left I hant been back since we have moved from our horsepital to
the metical College I am very well pleased with my move I hant got
much to rite to you there is no fresh news here only congress has
passed the act to furlow all sick and wounded soldiers home for not
more than 60 days but I expect they will soon gave me a furlow to my
company I expect there will be a good many leave here this eavening
September the 26. 1862 nobody went off yesterday eavening but will
go off this eavning the doctors has just been around there companys
(turn over) I want go to my company til nex week no how if I keep
mending I will go then I just now got a letter from lis she said they
were all well she said she had got a letter from dock and he said he
thought if he kept on the good side of his captain he would get a discharge I cant find out whether he is gone with the company or not
lis nor al Martin nary one never said I will send ann some appaviter
seed[44] tell her to send me word how she likes her dress rite to me what
the children said about there candy and so on I would be glad to see
you all but there is no chance for that til the war ends I hope it wont
bee long first the papers says there is a proposition made for peace[45]
I hope it will be made soon so we can come home and stay there un-
molested the ballance of our days rite soon when I leave here and get
to my company I will rite to you where to rite to I am afraid I shall be
bothered to get to my company I am still fatning and I hope these
lines may reach you the same rite what bill and carline is doing and
how manuel is doing and so on nothing more at present only remain
your afectionate husband til death

John W. Cotton

if me no mor on earth you see   to his wife at home
when you here of war remember me

[44] Arbor vita? Ann is the oldest child and nearly twelve years old. Her father's
messages indicate he considers her no longer a child.
[45] This is the first mention of peace rumors which increase as the war progresses.

October the 2 1862

Atlanta Ga Medical college horsepittol Dear wife it is with pleasure
that I take my pen in hand to rite you a few lines to let you no that I
am well and will leave here this eavning for my company there is several of the legion going with me but none of my company we will
start half past 7 oclock this eavning I rote a letter and put it in the
office las weak but I dont no whether you got it or not I have not received nary letter from you since you left here I got a letter from lis
the other day she said they wer all well I am very sorry to leave here
without hering from you and the children I dont no whether little
ginney is dead or a live but I hope she is well before this time and I
hope these few lines may find you all well and all of the connection
I am a fraid that when I leave here that I never will here from you all
again nor see you until the war ends if I never come back again I
want you to do the best you can for your self and the children lern
them to love you and obey you and try to lern them to bee good children and if I never return I want you to keep you land and such
things as you need and raise your children the best you can I don't
want you to bee uneasy[46] because I have rote this but bee of good
cheer hire manuel next year if you want him carry on your business as
if you never expected me at home I herd from general smith[47] he is
three hundred miles from chattanooga in kentucky at a little place in
thirty miles of louisville I rote to you before that my company left
knoxville on the 18 of september I dont expect they have got to smith
yet I expect that I shall bee bothered to get to them I hant herd from
them since they left knoxville[48] nor I dont no what they done with my
horse I dont expect I can get Ases clost to him I no I cant if they
have taken my horse with them if I cant I will try to sell them and
take the money to him if I can get there things are a heap cheaper
there than they are here there was a colonel here this morning and
he said the best of horses wer selling at one hundred and twenty five
dollars becon 3 cts per pound corn 30 cts floar 10 dollars a barrel
butter 10 cts chees 15 cts coffee 7 and 8 pounds to the dollar whickey
33 cts a gallon good shoes $1.25 cts to 7.00 dollars good boots five dol-
lars he says they are fatning thousands of pork and our men are living

46 Here is expressed his high ideals for his children but coupled with that is his
practical advice about his wife keeping her land.

47 General Kirby Smith.

48 For an account of the campaign of the Army of Tennessee into Kentucky see
Evans, *Confederate Military History* (Atlanta: Confederate Publishing Co., 1899)
VIII, Chapter 4.

as well as they can they get everything to eat they want to eat I wish I was there it will not bee worth while for you to rite to me any more until you here from me again I am so bothered that I dont no what else to rite to you dont bee uneasy about me if you dont here from me you may no I am doing the best I can for my self tho in distant lands I rome I will think the more about home if on yankey soil I bee dont think eyle ever forget the I had a great notion to come home but I believe I will give it out and try to go on to my company but I expect I will have to stop at noxville and I dont no how long if I have to stay there long I will rite to you I may rite any how John W Cotton to Mariah Cotton and children at home

Tennessee Camp Convalescence near Noxville Oct the 8 1862
Mariah Cotton dear wife it is with much pleasure that I take my pen in hand to rite you a few lines I am hapy to think that I still have the opportunity to rite you a few lines these few lines leave me well and I hope they will find you all the same I hope they may find little ginney fat and sassa I dont no what I would give to here from herr now or see you all again but we are a good ways apart and it is uncertain when we will meet again I am at the convalescent camp at Knoxville waiting for company to go with me to my company there is one of my company here and I expect we will start to the company soon about day after tomorrow. I will rite again when I leave here I don't no whether we can get to our company or not but we will go as far as we can I understand that the army is still moveing on north I received a letter from you just as I was leaving atlanta and did not have time to read it until I had to leave I was very glad to here that you all were well but little girl and was glad to here that you had got home safe and as well as you did I was afraid you would have to stop on the way with little ginney I hope she is now well and all of the rest of you they took my horse of and left me a foot but I have another one that belongs to the legion that I will ride unless the owner comes before I get off I had to go about twelve miles after him he belongs to a man that is at home there is several horses left here and he can ride him if he ever comes back I hant got nary letter from the company since I saw you Albert martin has gone home he left here the eavning I got there but I never saw him they are furlowing a great many of the sick home from here and discharging them too very fast but there is a many a one here that need it that dont get it I am moveing with plunket and others he ort to have a discharge he has partly lost his hereing if you want to rite to me direct your letter to lexington ken-

tucky our company may bee there yet I am to go from here there I will bee very glad to here from you if I should ever get there but I have a dangerous road to travoil for about two hundred miles I only have to hope that I will go threw safe I want you to pray for me that I may go threw safe to my company and threw the war til we have moved the yankeys back from our soil and peace is maid and that I may return safe home to you all again nothing more but remain your best friend John W. Cotton

John W. Cotton to Mariah Cotton Tennessee Camp Convalessents near Knoxville October the 9 1862 Dear wife I again have the pleasure to rite you a few lines to let you no that I am well and getting tolerable Stout again I hope these few lines may find you all well and doing well I hant much to rite to you I sent you a letter yesterday by mail but I will send this by hand ould mr hamd that lives down below he is going home on a furlow I dont no yet when I will leave here the adjutant talked yesterday of sending off about 100 men to day or tomarrow and sending me with them but there is a good many of them that they had started acomeing back not beeing able to make the march to there companys so they talk of not starting us yet a while I dont no when I will leave here there was lots of the legion come in here from comberland gap[49] this morning that wernt able to go with there companys they say they dont no where the cavalry is now but they are all gone to kentucky they say that it is oneny for just a few to go threw from cumberland gap on account of the bush whackers so I shant undertake to go to my company without a rite smart squad of men unless the officers force maby we are not fareing very well here but I can make out very well we get bread and beef and bread and a little rice there is a heap of grumbling in camps about not getting enough to eat but it is the way they mange it I have plenty I am messing with sam plunket and two others you no nothing about I hant any thing much to rite to you but if I could see you I could tell you a great deal I want you to rite to me as soon as you can when you get this letter and direct it to Noxville tennessee in care of captain M G. Slaughter hilliards legion cavalry battalion if I dont get it here it may go to the company by the time I do I am very sorry to think that I cant here from you all I would give almost any thing to here from lit-

<hr>

[49] Cumberland Gap was held by the Union forces under General George W. Morgan, a West Point classmate of Kirby Smith (Horn, *The Army of Tennesse,* 161-165).

tle ginney and here that she was well and all of you but it will be some
consolation to here from me nothing more at present but remain you
friend til death John W. Cotton

Camp Convealessents October the 15 1862
My Dear wife it is with much dissatisfaction that I again take my pen
in hand to rite you a few more lines to let you no that I am well as
common I am at the convealessent camps near knoxville and I am
doing tolerable well we dont get any thing hardly to eat but fresh
beef and flour we got a little bacon yesterday for the first time since
I have been here there is more grumbling here than I ever herd but
my mess makes out very well we bought a little bacon and we bought
a very nice cat fish this morning for one dollar there is but three in
my mess so I get plenty to eat I am as heavy as I ever was neary 167
pounds but I ant very stout yet I hope these few lines may reach you
all well and doing well I would bee very glad to here from you all I
want to here from little ginney very bad so I could no how she was
and all of the rest of you I shall be uneasy until I here from home
again I fear she has followed little cricket I cant help from shedding
tears when I think about her and think how bad I would miss her if
I were at home but I dont no that it will ever bee my happy lot to bee
there again to enjoy the privileges of beeing with the rest of you all
and enjoy our freedom as we have done before but I hope that we will
soon meet again I hope the war will not last mutch longer but I dont
see much chance now for peace the nuse has com here that the legion
has been in two fights the yankeys attacted them on there march from
cumberland gap to livingston but no streight news about the fight
there is 135 men of the legion here on the sick list but none of the
cavalry the officers here talk of sending off about for hundred men
from here to morrow that has got able to march if they go I shall go
with them but I think is uncertain about there starting for they hant
nere all got guns and it is uncertain about there getting them there is
none of the legion here that you ever new but elitia plunkey there
was 73 of them came in here last night that was left sick at cumberland
gap there was none of the cavalry left there I hant herd any thing from
my company yet this is three letters I have sent you since I have been
here I sent one by old man ham that lives away down towards reck-
ford and two by mail I have got ases close yet eye was over at the
horsepital just now and there was six dead men caried off from there
they dye from six to 8 a day there is 26 or 27 hundred men here and
not many able to go to there regiments there is a band of doctors here

now to examine the sick and furlow and discharge all they think need them brechenridges command is here and a great many others camped around her (turn over) there was a man come here from cumberland gap nite before last he says that hilliard left ordes there for the officers there not to let any more of the legion pass there but if any of them come there to turn them back here it is thought that he aims to take us down the country somewhere if they do come back I wish they would make haste and come before I leave here I dont no when I will leave here there was an old union man come in here to where some cavalry were camped and they tuck him up and he refused to take the oath[50] and they hung him three times before he tuck it and they then made him double quick it from there over here to our camps and our men gathered around him and develed him a good deal and then[51]   and then turned him loose and then made him leave in double quick time nothing more at present to rite to you but I hope these lines may find you all well no more at this time I will let you no when I leave here I remain you most affectionate husband til death John W. Cotton to Mariah Cotton and family there is a talk of the camps bin broke up if they are and they wont let me go to my company I will bee sent to atlanta or montgomery farewell I hope I may see you all soon and see little ginney fat and sassa and all of the rest

Knoxville Tennessee October the 18 1862
Mariah dear wife it is again that I take my pencil in hand to let you no that we are about to leave knoxville the order is to leave this eavning for kentucky these lines leave me well except the dirhoear but it is not hurting me mutch I hope these lines reach you all well and doing well I hant herd from you since I left atlanta and I am very uneasy about all and esspecialy little ginney I want to here from you all very bad but I am afraid it will along time before I can here from you all I was enhopes that I would get a letter from you before we left here there will bee 7 or 8 hundred in all cavalry and infantry we will all go to gether I have got the same horse yet that I got when I first came here and I will ride him threw if I have him to pay for but I ant much uneasy about that there is seven of our company here and lieutenant heerd our second lieutenant six of them were left here for

---

[50] Search to this point has not revealed an oath an "old union man" would take but probably it would be an oath of allegiance to the Confederacy.
[51] Manuscript torn.

cariers there is 211 of our battlion here to go along and a rite smart infantry and artilery I saw frank Carley this morning he come from strawbery plains yesterday he says he is not able to go with us but he is mending slowly he looks very well you must excuse my short letter and bad riting for I hant got much to rite now much time to rite it in for I have got to fix for leaveing here and eat dinner I want you to rite to me as soon as you get this letter if you call it one and direct you letter to lexinton kentucky in care of captain M G Slaughter Hilliands legion cavalry battalion I cant tell you how bad I want to see you all so I must close nothing more at present only remain you most affectionate husband til death

John W Cotton to Mariah Cotton

Knoxville Tennessee Ocotber 26, 1862 Dear wife I again take my pen in hand to rite you a few more lines to let you no I am well and am at knoxville and battalion is coming back here one company had got back and we are looking for our company every day what few of us that is here is doing very well and get plenty to eat and not much to do we have been detailed a few days to patrole the streets of knoxville we have had a beautiful spell of weather til last nite and today and we have had several pretty frosts it commenced snowing last nite and it has snowed over half the day the laves here is perfectly green and all covered with snow dock has started home but I reckon you will get a letter from him before you get this Strickland's company was here this weak but they are gone from here now I stayed with them one nite Mike and John were both well and fatter than I ever saw them I wey more than I ever did but I hant got the same action I use to have I think it is for want of exercise there is part of our company left us and gone to Steven company we were ordered to kentucky and we went about a mild and stopped to stay all nite and go on next morning next we had orders to start and before we got off we had orders not to go and we moved back clost to where we were before and nere here October the 27 Mariah I will rite you a few more lines our captan that commands our little squad will leave us today and go to his company but our first lieutenant is here with us and another lieutenant of the legion ther is three of our company here that the yankeys tuck prisoners and parolled them the talk now is that we will bee stationed at Comberlan gap this winter and I rather go any where else the whole army has left kentucky but I recien you have herd that there is more soldiers about here than I ever saw I hant got any news from you since I left Atlanta but I have looked for a letter from you for some time but I hant got nary one yet I want you to rite to me again as soon as you get these few lines direct your letter to knoxville to J. W. Cotton knoxville tennessee I may stay here til I get a letter from you and I may not stay here two days I want to git to my company very bad I am tired of being drug about by other officers I hant got much to rite to you it is not worth while to try to tell you how bad I want to see you all or here from you if I could here from you all and here that little ginney has go well and all of the rest of you I woul bee very glad to come home and see you all and see how things is going on and make arrangements for another year but there is no chance nw you must do the best yu can for your self and the children only remain your affectionate husband til death John W. Cotton to Mariah Cotton

Knoxville Tennessee November the 3 1862
Mariah Dear wife I once more take my pen in hand to rite you a few lines to let you no that I am well and doing tolerable well so fare as bodily health but I am distressed in mind I have not herd from you since I left atlanta you last letter was dated the 28 September which has been one month and six days you have no idea on how bad I want to here from you all for I cant here whether little ginney is dead or alive I want to hear from youall but I had much rather see you all but I dont no when I will get to see you all again there is several of our boys gone home now and our camptain is gone home and Joe leavnett and bill adkins that lives above Attaline they left here yesterday morning they have gone home after clothing I want you to send me a coat and my nit shirt by bill adkins and a letter and if dock has got home tell him to rite to me bill adkins was here nite before last at our camp but I did not get to see him I have been off on detached service for six days and just got in last nite there was 16 of us went away over in to north Carolina to drive some beef cattle out of the mountains about 75 miles from here and about 25 miles rite threw the mountains and fourteen miles atrail was and the worst mountains and the worst trail that ever I saw there is but one house for 25 miles our horses had to do three days and nites on twenty nubbins of corn but we had plenty to eat we brought out 70 head of cattle if I could see you I could tell you a heap more about our trip over ther but I wont rite no more about it turn over I heard from assa and bill lessley last nite they are at cumberland gap all is well bill is sorter punny but able to bee about floid googame is here now he is rite from the company he says our company will bee down here in

aday or two our lieutenant says he is goint to start to them tomorrow
if they dont come if he can get off it is not known yet where we will
take up winter quarters I have no notion where we will stay ther is a
great deal of shifting about of soldiers now our captain is gone home
and our men say they dont think he will ever come back any more
Mariah I want you to send me 25 or 30 dollars of money by bill adkins
wit the other things for I hant got but $9 and 25 cts and I dont no
when we will draw any money for our service and I dont want to get
out of money for I mite need it very bad rite in the letter you send by
him how much you send to me and rite about things in general how
you all are and how you are getting on and how your stock is doing
and how manuel is geting along gathering corn and soweing grain
and son billy brown is very poor making a trip to kentucky and
back and then to north carolina and back has worsted him and doing
on no feed apart of the time I hant much to rite to you I have a bad
way to rite these lines leave me well and hop they find you enjoying
the same blessing nothing more at present but remain you affectionate
husband til death

John W. Cotton

When you rite your letters to Knoxville tennessee in care of Captain
M. G. Slaughter Hilliards legion unless I rite to you to direct them
some where else

Camp Baker Tennessee   November 8th 1862
Mariah Cotton dear wife now take my pen in hand to rite you a few
lines to let you no that I am well and fat as a bare I have been hartier
than I ever was in my life I can eat anything that comes before me I
am happy to tell you that I have got with my company again I got
with them yesterday morning and was glad to see all of the boys and
they appeared glad to see me they all are very glad they got out of kentucky they say they saw many hard times part of the time they were
gone and nerly all of them suffered a good deal of the dirhear I will
put this letter in with asa and I reckon he will rite all about there trip
the boys are all about but aheap of them are complaining rite smart
billy martin is complaining rite smart to day I hant got but a few
words to rite to you but I thought I would rite a few to let you no I
was well I hope these few lines may find you all well and doing well
I was very glad to here that you were doing so well you said all you
laked was me I wish I was with you but it may bee a long time before
we see each other again if ever but I am not out of hart yet I think I

shall come back again to stay with you all and enjoy the freedom we
are now fighting for I hope I will come home soon I dont want you
to get out of hart about me but enjoy yourself the best you can I could
not help shead tears when I red your letter the other day you said you
got worse about the loss of little cricket I shall dread to come home for
I no I shall miss her so much she will not bee there to fondle on my
nees with the rest of the little fellows but I try to study about it as
little as possible for I no she is a great deal better off than I am we
should not grieve that she is gone to a better world than this and gone
where she never can come to us but we can go to her I cant help
sheading tears ever time I get to studying about you all it now nearly
dark and I hant got no candle the next letters you send send them
without paying the postage on them and then if I dont get them I
wont have to pay for them we are camped today ten miles below knoxville and it is thought we will go from there to murfeys borough they
are expecting a big fite there before long and at nashville too some
thinks that we will not take up winter quarters atall but keep fighting
all winter if they dont soon stop and let our horses rest we will soon
bee afoot for our horses looks very bad but my horse looks better than
he did a few days ago I want you to do the best you can for yourself
and the children and no bee uneasy about me for I am doing very
well at present I hope little ginney will bee well by the time you get
this letter I am going to try to come home betwext this and christmas
if I see any chance but I want you to make your arrangements as
though you never looked for me nothing more at present only remain
you affectionate husband til death John W. Cotton

Camp Baker Tennessee November the 15. 1862
Mariah Cotton my dear loveing and affectionate wife it is with great
pleasure I take my pen in hand to rite you a few lines to let you no
that I have received your kind and affectionate letter and very glad to
here from you all and to here that you were all well and doing so well
I am very glad to think you dont like nothing but me[52] and I am very
glad to here that little ginney is getting fat and sassa again for I have
suffered a great deal of uneasyness about her. I am better satisfied
than I have been since you left me at atlanta the other letter that I
got from you gave me great satisfaction but this one gave me more I
have received two letters from you since I come to knoxville one dated
the 25 October and one the 30 of october I begun to think that I wernt

[52] This must have warmed his lonely heart!

agoing to get nary one from you but I new you had rote to me before that time I rote to you that we were agoing to leave here the next day but we are here yet 10 miles below knoxville we may leave here tomorrow and we may not leave here in a week or two the officers say that we will go to murfeysborough from here and from there to bridgeport 18 miles below Chattanooga lieutenant beerd has rote to the men that was sent home after clothing to take them to bridgeport if you get this letter before adkins come back you need not send me any money for we have drawn $72 a piece so I have got money aplenty now you need not send me any thing but a coat we have not got them close that you sent us yet but I recken the the men that were sent home after close will get back and bring them to us it is thought that our captain wont never come back to us any more and our first leiutenant has allredy resigned and our second lieutenant talks of resigning if they all resign it will leave the company in a very bad fix our battalion is all together now for the first time since I left them our battlion is taken from the legion and detached to general henly smiths division for his body guard we will not be apt to stay here long for they are expecting a big fight at murfeysborough and we will be apt to go there soon it is near nashville tennessee these lines leave me well and asa is well william lessley is complaining some I hope these few lines may reach you all well and still doing well rite to me as soon as you get this letter rite all of the news every thing is very hy here we have to pay one dollar and fifty cts per bushel for corn and forty cts per pound for pork from ten to fifteen cts per pound for beef and everything else according I hant mutch to rite to you rite to me how your stock is doing and if you have sold any pork yet and if you have killed any beef yet or sold any on foot and what you got for it I want to come home very bad but I dont no when I will get to come to see you all dont get out of hart I think I will come some time or other it is not worth while to try to tell how bad I want to see you all dont be uneasy about me and I will not be no uneasier than I can help no mor at present only remain your loving husband til death John W. Cotton

November the 16 we are now packing up to leave for bridgeport direct you next letter to John W cotton bridgeport Alabama in care of mr M. G. Slaughter if Adkins dont leave before you get these few lines send me a letter by him fare well my dear wife

Chattanooga Tennessee   November 23th 1862
Mariah dear wife it is again that I have the opportunity to rite you a
few lines to let you no that I am well and hope you are enjoying the
same good blessing we are now camped at Chattanooga at the same
place where we were when we left here to go to Knoxville we will
leave here this morning to go to a place called Jasper about 30 miles
we may stay there a while but I dont no how long when you get this
letter rite to me a direct you letter to bridgeport Alabama it is only
5 miles from Jasper they are all having there letters directed to bridgeport I hant got but little time to rite this morning it was late last nite
when we got here and we are now fixing up to leave here we had a
very pleasant trip down here if I could see you I could tell you a heap
but I hant got the time to rite much when we get stopped I will try to
rite more when I get more time I thought the maby I would get to
come home before Christmas but is very uncertain now when I will get
to come we may go to murfeysborough and have a fite there is a talk of
a fite there before long our company is improving in health a great
deal Asa and William is well the company is about but some of them
are complaining some our horses are improving a little my horse is
mending some but he has got a sore back we have had plenty for them
to eat ever since we left Knoxville nothing more at present I remain
your affectionate husband til death John W. Cotton
Dont bee uneasy about me fore I am doing very well

Winchester Tennessee   December the 1 1862
Mariah Cotton dear wife it is again that I take my pen in hand to rite
you a few lines to let you no that I am still well and enjoying good
health but I am not satisfyed in mind I hand got nary letter from you
in some time the last I got was rote the 30 of october I would like
very much to here from you all and to no that you were still doing
well I want to come home very bad but but it is a bad chance now
and the chance dont get any better I dont no whether I will get to
come home atall or not but that dont keep from wanting to come I
hant got them close you sent me yet but I am looking for them now
every day the men that was sent home after them has not got back yet
there time was out yesterday I would bee very glad to get my yarn
shirts[53] now we are having some bad weather now we had a powerful
rain last nite and it is cold and cloudy today but we have got a good
tent and we don't mind rain when we are stationed at a place so we

---

[53] Could this be a sweater?

can stretch our tent we got here last nite we left camp Jasper the next day after I rote to you before I dont no how long we will stay here but I dont think we will stay long I think we will go from here to murpheys borough or nashville I think they are fixing for a fite at one of them places before long I was in hopes a while back that the war would end this christmas or some time this winter but I dont see any chance now for it to end soon but we must live in hopes if we dy in dispare[54] I dont dread the fighting that I will have to do all I hate is having to stay from home and being exposed to the weather I dont want you to bee uneasy about me for I am fatter than ever was in my life I way 179 pounds I have out fattened any body you every saw since you left me I hope these few lines may find you all enjoying as good health as I am I want you to cary on your business as if you never expected to see me any more do the best you can and you will please me if I dont come home you must make your arrangements for another year and the best you can if any body want to rent the jacobs place[55] rent it to them for what ever you can I hant got much to rite to you tell wash to rite to me and all of the rest and I want you to rite but I dont no where to tell you to direct you letter to for I dont no where we will go to from here I will rite to you again soon nothing more at present but remain your loving husband til death   John W Cotton to Mariah Cotton

Tennessee Camped to stay all nite December 9th 1862
My dear beloved wife it is again I take my pen in hand to answer a letter that I recieved last nite it was dated the 15 of november I was glad to here from you but I was sorry to here that the children was sick and had been sick but I am glad that they are no worse off I was sorry to here that little ginney had been sick again and I was sorry to here that dock had not gott any better of his hereing I got a letter from him too with yourn I was very glad to here that everything was going on as well as what they were you said you did not no what you would do for salt I am afraid you will have to do without it salt is very scarce up here[56] we have been stationed at winchester tennessee but we left there yesterday morning we are now on the march to

---

[54] A bit of folk philosophy.

[55] On January 18, 1838, he had bought 80 acres for $220 from Joseph Jacobs and wife, Elizabeth Jacobs (Record of Deeds (Coosa County) Book J., Old Series, p. 374).

[56] For the importance of salt see Ella Lonn, *Salt as a Factor in the Confederacy*, New York: W. Neale, 1933.

readysville about 15 miles from nashville there is a big fite expected
there in a few days if we have one I expect all of our battalion will
bee in it there is some of our men running away and going hom there
is fore that went home without leave has come back they were court
marshaled and put under gard for ten days and live on bread and
water and deduct there wages for one month there is two of our company gone now floid goodgame and McBarnet our army is in a heep
of confusion and mitely out of hart a man told me today in manches-
ter that there had been as many as 50 of there briggade deserted in
one nite[57] I could rite a heap but when I go to rite I cant think of
half I want to rite if I could see you all I could tell you all a heap I
did not much like to leave winchester when we did for we got as much
corn as our horses could eat and enough to eat our selves I wanted
to stay there til we got our close we have not got them yet they are
at bridgeport on the tennessee river and they cant get them across on
account of there beeing so many clothing and commessaries to cross
and soldiers they wont get across before the fifteenth of this month
it will bee around christmas before we get our close but the man that
started with them will stay with them til we get them we have had
some as cold weather here as I nearly ever saw in alabamma the roads
is very muddy and hard frozen smiths hole command is rite ahead of
us going to the same place they say the yankes are advancing on us
from nashville you said you want me to give all of the advice I could
I dont no how to advise you unless I new how how every thing was
going on you can tell what is best to do I was sorry you sold your corn
for I think if you had kept it till spring you could got two dollars as
easy as one[58] but I dont blame you for selling it for I no you done the
best you could if you do the best you can I will bee satisfyed you
never said whether you had hired manuel or not nor whether you
had sold your beef or not I want to come home the worst perhaps I
want to come home to see the children before they forget me nothing
more at present I remain your affectionate husband till death John
W Cotton

[57] Two studies of Confederate desertions are Ella Lonn, *Desertion During the Civil* War, New York: The Century Co., 1928, and Bessie Martin, *Desertion of Alabama Troops from the Confederate Army,* New York: Columbia University Press, 1932.

[58] In all probability she could have got more than $2.00 for in May, 1863, corn was selling for $3.00 (Walter L. Fleming, *Civil War and Reconstruction in Alabama,* New York: Columbia University Press, 1905, p. 180) .

[December 10, 1862]

A few lines to dock well dock you said you had rote to me two or three times and had not got nary one from me I rote to you about drawing you money and directed it to your pap I drew three months wages for you but not competation money[59] and I have got it yet I got a letter from you and mariah last nite you rote to me that you had drawn 3 months wages the same that I drawed for you dont say any thing about it[60] and maby we will make that much for no body dont no here that you draws any at atlanta I was glad to here from you but was very sorry to here that you had not got no better of your hereing you wanted me to see if the captain was will ing for you to have a transfer he is gone home and some of the company thinks he wont come back any more beerd has resigned and gone home we will have and election for lieutenant before long[61] some of the boys wants me to run I may run and and I may not starne is our commander now I want you to stay at home if you can I hant much to rite to you nor much chance for I have to rite on my nee by fire lite and not litewood I got the five dollars that Timmone owed you he has got a discharge and gone home nothing more at present I remain your friend til death John W Cotton Dec the 10 these lines leaves us all well but norten he is not very will the the company is in very good health I am still fatning nothing more

Tennessee 4 miles west of Reedysville Dec the 12 1862

My dear wife it is again that I take my pen in hand to rite you a few lines to let you know that I am well and to let you no that I have got the close and mones you sent to me by bill adkins he got here last nite but he did not bring all of the close he started with ten he brought mine and aases and bills and some others the box of pervisions you and nan sent and the other close was left at knoxville and a man with them they could not get them threw but I rote to you in another letter but I will send this with the others I could not get to mail them when I rote them so I will send them together   I am well pleased with

[59] Mr. Peter A. Brannon of the Department of Archives and History, Montgomery, says this is "commutation" money in payment for clothing for themselves and feed for their horses which they had had to provide.

[60] This seems to be the only instance of doubtful honesty in all the letters; in all other instances Cotton was scrupulously careful to do the right thing.

[61] Officers from majors up were usually appointed by the governor but all company officers were elected by the troops (*Statutes*, I, 223; E. Merton Coulter, *The Confederate States of America 1861-1865*, Baton Rouge: Louisiana University Press, 1930, p. 329). Cotton may not have run for office at this time for Bill Atkins was elected (December 21, 1862). He did run later but was defeated (May 26, 1863).

the close you sent me the coat is some too little the vest does very well
I would not take nothing for my necktie   I found a very good pare of
gloves yesterday when I rote that other letter I did not expect to get
my close til about christmas but I have got them now you said something about my aald coat somebody stold it from me betwen atlanta
and dalton when I went to knoxville I hant much to write to you now
we are stationed 4 miles from reedyville and 8 miles from murfreys
borough I dont no how long we will stay here but you may direct you
letters to murfreys borough I hope these few lines may find you all
enjoying good health and doing well I will rite again soon rite as soon
as you get this letter nothing more at present but remain your affectionate husband til death   John W Cotton

Tennessee Belirford County December the 17 1862
Dear beloved wife and children once more I tak my pen in hand to
rite you a few lines to let you no that I am well and hope these few
lines may find you all well and doing well our company has got all
of there close but one box it got lost on the way and nobody dont no
how adkins left the close with ginks at Chattanooga and he brought
them to murfeysborough the box that was lost only had three pars of
pant three shirts one pare of drawers and our sach of fruit or box of
pervisions came safe we were very glad to get them but we did not
much need the bacon we got the box last nite and we made the apples
and potato get further and we had a setting up mess of pees for dinner
to day we hant eat much of our butter yet we tryed it a little we
drawed seven days rashons this morning we drawed flour bacon molasses sugar rice and soap and a little salt we got plenty to eat now and
has all the time our horses get more corn than they can eat but no
fodder they dont pull much fodder in this cuntry and it is very scarce
we are at the same place we were at when I rote to you before I rote
to you before about getting new close and where we were we are fore
milds from reedy ville and eight from murfeys borough and about 30
miles from nashville the yankeys are betwixt murfeysborough and
nashville they were fighting over there yesterday but we dont not how
they made it we dont here much war news here you here a heap more
than we do (it was reported here that they had stopped our letters
from going home but I here it disputed I dont think it is so I will start
this letter any how I will send you a few flax seed) it is reported here
that there is a great many soldiers deserting on both sides and I here
a heap say that is all the way to make peace but I dont think so I
think it is the worst thing that our men has every done for the South

there has several of our men deserted from the battalion I want that
to bee the last thing that I do I would bee glad to come home to see
you all but I dont want to come without furlow and there is no
chance to get a furlough now for the major wont let nobody have a
furlough mariah you rote that you wanted me to come home and make
arrangement for another year I would bee glad to come but I cant so
you must make your own arrangement I no you are at a great loss to
no what to do but you can see what is needed better than I can and
me not nowing how things is going on I think if you can hire manueal
again you can do very well til I can come home if you have more
money than you need lend it out if you can get good notes for it if
you need any thing you need not bee afraid to by it I dont need the
money you sent to me but I will try to take care of it you never rote
what you had done with your beef asa got a letter from nan nite before last rote the 2 of december I hant got nary one rote since adkins
lef there asa is well but william Lessley is very porley with his old
disease rite to me and direct you letters to Murfeys borough we may
stay here a rite smart while you dont no how bad I want to see you
all and bee at home to see how things are going on nothing more at
present I remain your loving husband til death farewell at present
John W Cotton

Tennessee Camped to stay all night December 21th 1862
dear beloved wife it is with pleasure that I rite you a few lines to let
you no that I am still well and I hopes these few lines find you all
well and doing well and enjoying yourselves the best you can I want
to come to see you very bad and make arrangements for another year
but we are now on the march from reedyville to knoxville we have
been on the march three days we are now nearn Sporty (?) Tennessee
we will bee some 8 or 10 days more on the march as soon as I get to
Knoxville I will rite again if not before direct your next letters to
Knoxville we will stay there a while some thinks we will stay there all
the winter the news is here that the yankeys are going to Mississippi
river and all the soldiers is leaving from about murfeysborough but
brags armey they have give out fighting their I cant find out what
they are moving us to Knoxville for I dont see no chance to get a
feurlow now but when I get to Knoxville I will try to get a furlow we
have elected bill adkins for our lieutenant he says he will do all he
can to get me a furlow he is elected in beerds place till he comes back
I hant much to rite and not much chance to rite I am riting by a fire
made out of rails and all most no pen I hope you will do well till I

get to come home to make a crop I would send you some advice but I
dont no how things is going on you must do the best you can and I
will be satisfied you rote to me to give you all the advice I could but I
dont no what to advise you to do for the best only try to take care of
what little you have got and see that manuel dont waste nothing I am
in hopes you will hire him again for I dont no any other chance for
you to make a crop pay oald man brown for this years wages[62] and pay
your blacksmithing if you have money enough tell all that wants to
rite to us to rite to us at Knoxville William Lessley is better now asa
left us at reedyville to go after some cattle about forty miles and he
hant overtuck us yet it is uncertain when he will get to us nothing
more at present but remain your affectionate husband till death John
W Cotton to his life.

Tennessee Camped at kingston December 26th 1862
Mariah Dear wife it is once more that I take my pen in hand to rite
you a few more lines to let you no where I am and to let you no that I
am well and doing well the boys are most all well william is better
than he was when he was when I rote before asa hant got to us yet I
am looking for him we are at kingston we got here yesterday we will
stay here a while the major got orders to stay here a while til he got
further orders we may stay here some time they say ther is three cases
of small pox here in the horsepital but I dont here much said about it
but there is several of the boys beeing nocilated I hant much to rite
to you only to let you no that I am well I tryed this morning to get a
furlow I got it rote and lieutenant otery sined it and then the major
would not approve it he said it was against general smiths orders so
you may guess what my chance is to come home I am very sorry that
I cant get to come home I no you are at a loss to no what to do with
your farm I am afraid you hant got ould manuel hired again if you
hant you must try to get somebody to tend your land for I dont no
what you will do if you dont get somebody to make some corn for you
I have all most give out the wars closeing this winter this is one
chrisman that I wont see much fun nor drink much eggnog but we got
some brandy chrismas eave and we had a chrismas dram but no nog
we have a heap of gard duty to do camp gard and picket gard on our

---

62 One wishes the wages paid for Manuel were given. The only indication of the
sum is later (January 20, 1864) when Mariah Cotton had to give 150 bushels of
corn for him. This seems to be much more than formerly paid for in two letters
her husband deplores the large amount she had to pay.

march I rote to you since we have been on the march from reedyville to this place we have been on the road 8 days we have beautiful weather on our march but it is raining some this eavning tell dock to rite to me and let we no what he is doing and I will rite to him when I can tell lis to rite some too and you must still rite direct your letters to knoxville the major got a dispatch from there and he wont tell what was in it so we dont no what will bee done next he has just got it I dont care much where we go to no how for I cant get to come home no how it ant worth while to try to tell you how bad I want to see you all I would like to come home before the children forget me nothing more at present only remain your affectionate husband til death John W Cotton

December the 31st 1862   Tennessee kingston
Mariah Cotton Dear wife it is again I take the opportunity to rite you a few lines to let you no that I am well and the company is in tolerable good health there is but 2 sick Sam Jacobs is sick it is thought that he will die the other men not very bad off I am sorry to say to you that I hant herd from you since bill adkins left there I am very anxious to here from you all asa hant got back to us yet but I am looking for him every day it is time he had come back I have rote to you twice since he has been gone he has been gone from the company 2 weeks I hant much to rite only to let you no that I am well I hope these few lines may find you all well and doing well I want to see you all very bad but there is no chance to come home yet the most of the people here thinks that the war will come to a close about Spring we have a heap of duty to do now there ant no troops here but us and we have to boat our corn down the river three miles and we have to stand gard over prisoners that are under gard for going home without furlough and stand picket and go out on a scout every day I went out nite before last on a scout with twenty more men and we rode 25 miles after nite we rode til 3 o'clock in the nite we went 17 miles from camp we have moved two miles from kingston right in the fork of the Tennessee and clinch river we went into some camp that some other soldiers had just left we have good chimleys to put out tent to and good fire places we are very well fixed to take the winter the major says we may stay here all the winter and may not very long but he says the prospect is a good for us to stay here a good while the legion is ordered here it will bee here soon one of the colonels was here this morning he said they stayed in 8 miles of here last nite I am anxious to here from home to know how you have

made your arrangements for another year I am afraid you hant got nobody to make a crop for you if you dont get somebody to make a crop for you I dont no what you will do tell dock to rite to me and let me no what he is doing direct your letters to kingston Mariah if you have got any more money than you need lend it out if you can get good notes for it[63] I have swaped bill off and give $30 to boot he was rode down he had the thumps ever day I rode him I have got a big sarel horse 9 year oald next spring he is as large as oald and a better riding horse I hated to swap bill off but I saw he was going to give out if he did not get rest I think I have got a good handy horse he is in good order nor nothing more at present but remain your affectionate husband til death

John W Cotton

I will send you some seed called pie melons plant them like a water melon

---

[63] Note the repeated instrucitons that indicate Cotton had an eye for business and at the same time a feeling of dependence on the land.

1863

Tennessee Camp Kingston January 7th 1863
Mariah Cotton Dear wife it is with pleasure I take my pen in hand to
rite you a few lines to let you no that I am well but not satisfyed I
have not got nary letter from you since adkins left home nor hant even
herd from you since he got here I want to here from you and the children very bad and I want to see you all a heap worse but dont know
when I will get to see you all again I rote to you about trying to get
a furlow and cood not get it the major got orders a few days ago not
to sine no furlows under no circumstances what ever unless the doctor
said they would dye if they stayed in camp so you may no that my
chance is bad to come home we have herd here that there is a talk of
stopping women from riting to there husbands in the war when ever
that comes to pass and I know it to bee so I am comeing home and I
will stay when I get there there is rite smart of excitement about it
here I wont come by myself our batalion is formed into a regiment with
a georgia battalion a man by the name of Good[64] is our Colonel and
slaughter Lieutenant Colonel our captain hant come back yet slaughter
is commander of the poste here I just got back from a scout last nite
we went up towards clinton and the salt works we were in 8 miles of
clinton 20 miles from knoxville the news come here that the yankeys
had taken our forces at big creek gap and had come on threw but we
could not here anything of it up where we went so it must not bee so
we here that our men have whiped the yankeys bad at murfeysborough[65] there is a great talk here of peace beeing mad about spring I
hope they may make peace about spring or before for I want to come
home and see what you all are doing I would like to no whether you
have got any body to make a crop for you or not I want to come home
time enough to make a crop myself Mariah you may tell dock the officers have mad out the paroles to advance two months wages but they

64 Charles T. Goode from Georgia. This is the 10th Confederate Cavalry which
was formed "by consolidating Goode's battalion (the 19th Georgia Cavalry) and
Slaughter's of Hilliard's legion" in December, 1862 (W. Brewer, *Alabama: Her history, Resources, War Record and Public Men from 1540 to 1870,* Montgomery:
Barrett and Brown, 1872, p. 693).

65 Murphreesboro was considered a victory for the Confederates but on January
4 General Bragg retreated (Horn, *The Army of Tennessee,* 210). There is a detailed
account of the battle in *Confederate Military History,* VIII, 57-77.

wont draw no money for nobody that is not present tell him that the money that I drawed for him before I will have to pay back to the company if he had not told adkins I mite have kept it but I will have to pay it back to the officers tell dock that there is an order issued[66] for all soldiers absent from camps to return to camps by the 20 of this month we may stay here some time I think the prospect good to stay here sometime direct your letters to kingston tennessee I would like to no the reason I dont get no letters from you I no you must rite to me I am looking for a letter from you every day but get none asa and porter is well nothing more at present only remain your affectionate friend til death John W Cotton

Kingston Tennessee January the 13 1863 Mariah dear wife it is with much dissatisfaction that I rite you a few lines to let you no that I am well and hope these few lines may find you all enjoying good health I am well but not satisfyed I hant got nary letter from you yet I hant herd a word from you since adkins got back I am afraid the mail is stopped there has been such talk here as there stopping our women from riting to us if it is so and I find it out I will be as certain to come home as I live and I want bee all there is lots of men says the same we are doing tolerable well at present we get plenty to eat and plenty corn for our horses but no hay nor fodder I am afraid we wont get plenty long there is two many of us together we are formed into a regiment good is our colonel and slaughter is our lieutenant Colonel and Rudolph major good had a battalion from georgia and they put ourn and his together and made a regiment I hant got much to rite to you we have rite smart of picket and scouting to do and camp gard duty to do and we have to go up the river from two to seven miles and bring it down on a flat for our horses I would like very well to here from dock and here how he is getting and what he is doing I would like to here from you all and know how you all are getting along and I would bee very glad to hear how you have made your arrangements for another year I am uneasy for fear you hant go nobody to make a crop for you I cant hear nothing from you all I am a fraid you hant hired old manuel again I believe I want to here from home worse than I ever did or ever have since I have been in the

66 This evidently was an order from the war department for no such action was taken by Congress. The Confederate Congress, however, in this period took repeated action on the question. See *Journal of the Congress of The Confederate States of America,* Washington: Government Printing office, III, 152, 171, 222, 291 and many others.

service and it is not any use to talk of comeing home for there is no
chance for a man to come home unless the doctor thinks he will dye
if he stays in camps I think if I could come home and see how every
thing was going on I could stay in camps better satisfyed than I ever
have for I am getting more use to staying from home but I am very
much dissatisfyed to staying more and will bee until I here from you
all I ant in no humor to rite this morning so I will come to a close I
remain your affectionate husband til death   John W Cotton to Mariah Cotton

Kingston Tennessee January 19th 1863
Dear wife it is with much pleasure I take my pen in hand to answer
your kind letter I received a letter from you last thursday and was
very glad to hear from you all one time more and I was glad to here
that you were doing so well You said all you liked was me at home it
gave me much satisfaction to hear that you were doing so well   I
would like very well to be at home with you but I cant tell when that
will be our happy lot to meet at home again I am in hopes the war
will come to a close towards spring it is thought by a great many that
there will bee a change now soon for the better you need not look for
me til you see me but I am comeing as soon as I get the chance   I was
glad to here that you had hired manuel again for I was afraid you
would not get nobody to make a crop for you this year at all we are at
kingston yet and there is a good many more troops acomeing in here
John Tramels company is here   it has been here several days I saw
Mike and John this morning o they were well they are camped in
about a mild and a half from here homes waldrop is here now I dont
think we can all stay here long on account of getting corn   we cant
get corn long unless they brote it to us with a steam boat   we will not
have so much duty to do now as we have had these troops comeing
in will do apart of our duty   we hant drawn our money yet we sent
the paroles[67] to knoxville twice but it come back as we sent it the
major said he would try to get the pay master to come here and pay us
you had to pay very hy for salt to salt your meet it looks like paying
the worth of your meet to get it salted[68] there was some of your hogs
that did not way very well   it is thought that bacon will be very hy
I think you have lost smartly by selling your corn when you did   I

[67] Pay rolls.
[68] In South Alabama salt was worth in Confederate money from $80 to $95 a sack
(Fleming, *Civil War and Reconstruction*, 180).

here that corn is worth two dollars and a half per bushel about pinkneyville captain slaughter has not come back yet but some of the boys
are looking for him he sent us word he would start back the 15 of this
month   I reckon you herd asa has lost his horse he hant got nary
nother yet there is several of our boys without horses and it is a bad
chance to get any more here   I cant think of any thing else to rite
now only to tell you that I am well and much better satisfyed than I
was when I rote before all of the boys are well   I hope these few lines
may find you all enjoying the same good blessing   I must say some
thing about the children   I was glad to here that little ginney was
doing so well   I hope she will walk soon   I am sorry that sweet[69] cant
talk   I will bet that babe[70] can talk about that candy paw sent him
and all of the rest tell them I will bring them some more when I come
home if I can get it   I want to see the little fellows very bad tell
bunk[71] he must get that eye strait before I get hom and tell bud[72] he
must make haste and get big enough to plough tell ann[73] she must not
get maried til I come home nothing more I remain your affectionate
husband til death

John W Cotton

Home home sweet home my long
loved home way down in Alabemer

Home home I hope when I get home
I will bee out of hering of wars clammer

[69] Andrew C. L. T. Cotton (born April 22, 1860) died relatively young, February
28, 1876 (family Bible).

[70] Jefferson Davis Cotton was born March 11, 1859 (family Bible) and lived until
September 15, 1930. After his father died in 1866 he went back to Coweta County,
Georgia, to live with his grandfather, William Hindsman. He married Nancy
(Nannie) Webb from Coweta County on December 24, 1882 (*Marriage Records*,
Coweta County) and for many years lived on a farm which was a part of the origi-
nal Cotton homestead. On it is the Cotton-Hindsman family cometery where Wil-
liam Hindsman, his wife Nancy Cotton Hindsman and several others are buried.
Mrs. Jeff Cotton, now 90 but hale and hearty and with a mind clear as a bell with
her only child, Miss Myrtice Cotton, are now living in Moreland, Georgia.

[71] William Cary Cotton was born April 21, 1856, (family Bible), but died young
leaving two sons, William and Weaver Allen. His wife was Miss Nannie Carlile
(Mrs. Nannie Cotton). There is a difference of opinion about the eye: Mrs. Ludie
Porch says her mother, "little ginny", told her he had one vividly blue eye and
one as equally black; Mrs. Nannie Cotton remembers nothing about the color but
said he had a bad squit in one eye that was caused by a knife injury.

[72] John Michael Cotton, (March 30, 1855-1930) was the first child born in Alabama. He became a carpenter by trade, went back to Coweta County, married first
Fannie Webb, sister of Nannie Webb, and later a Mrs. Skidmore. Three brothers—
these last two named and James Weaver, born during the war—died in 1930 within

Kingston Tennessee February the 2 1863

Dear wife I take my pen in hand to rite you a few more lines to let you no that I am well only I have a very bad cold but it ant hurting me much I hope these few lines may find you all well and doing well I red a letter from you last nite dated the 14 of January Jim Brady brought it it had been here a weak before I got here I just got back from kentucky last nite we were gone up there ten days I would have rote sooner if I had been in camps it has been about two weaks since I rote to you I rite one time ever weak when I am in camp I have got only two letters from you since Bill adkins come back with our close you rote that you had hired manuel again I was glad to hear that for I was afraid you would not get nobody to make a crop for you I was glad to here that you were all well and doing well I was not very well pleased when I herd what you had to give for salt enough to salt your pork I was glad you had the money to pay for it I think if time dont change you can make it back when you go to sell your bacon I would like to bee at home now to eat some sausage and ribs and backbones but we have fresh meat a plenty now the boys had just been out when I got back and killed two hogs so we have fresh meat a plenty when ever we dont draw rashions a plenty we go out and kill a hog we wont suffer as long as we can find any hogs we are all getting so we dont care much for nothing they say we are ordered to the Cumberland gap and lots of the boys says they wont go they say if the command starts there they will start home there is some leaving constant I am going to try again to get a furlow but I am a fraid it will bee a bad chance John Tramel has furlowed twenty seven men home they are furlowing a heap of there regiment maybe it will come to my time after while I would like very well to come home and see you all and see how things are going on at home and see how manuel is getting on with his crop and show him how to plant his crop and see to things in general you rote to me to rite all the advice I could all I have got is for you to enjoy yourself the best you can and go to see your neighbors and go to meeting you rote to me you not been to meeting since I left home I think you could enjoy yourself better if you would go to meeting and go to see your neighbors you need not bee uneasy bout me for I will

nine months (Mrs. Nannie Cotton, Miss Myrtice Cotton to Lucille Griffith, June 10, 1950). There is a picture of these three men made when they were in their sixties that show a remarkable similarity in appearance, so much so that, the family calls it the "picture of the triplets."

73 Ann was born in Georgia, December 16, 1850. Little is known of her other than that she married Willis Burks, a neighbor (Mrs. Nannie Cotton).

bee sure to take care of myself I can make out where any body else can lieutenant Beerd has come back to us and lieutenant Sterns has resigned and is going home the Captain has not come back yet he says he cant come back til spring and if they try to make hime come back before spring he will resign a heap of our men come in while I was gone and we have some new recruits asa said John Tramel was here the other day to get dock transfered to his company he will be transfered to that company and then he will get a discharge I will tell you something of our trip to kentucky we had a bad trip of it it rained on us a heap and snowed on us two days and nites and it was very bad traveling in the snow and the roads were very mudy they are the worst roads that ever I saw we went to Monticello kentucky one hundred and twenty miles we saw no enemy only some bush whackers we shot one of them and wounded him very bad and we tuck one yankey recruiting officer we got one man taken by the bush whackers and one drowned and one shot accidentally but not dangerous we had about 300 men with us if I could see you I could tell you a heap but I must bring my letter to a close asa is complaining with the dirhoea and porter is rite bad off with his ould complaint you said you wanted to send Ann to school[74] you may send her if you can do without her nothing more John W Cotton

Kingston Tennessee February 3 1863
Dear wife and children I will rite you a few lines to send to you by mr. gray he is coming home and I will send you a few lines to let you no that I am well and hope these few lines may find you all enjoying the same like blessing I hope you are all doing well I will not say much about coming home for they say there is no chance to get a furlow atall you must do the best you can til I do come there is a heap of talk about peace among the officeers I hope it will soon be made and that soon for I have been under an overseer about as long as I want to bee and I have been away from home a heap longer than I wanted to bee you said you wanted me and mike to have our likenesses drawn and send it to you I would like have mine drawn but there ant nobody here to draw it[75] and mike is gone but I told you about that in an-

[74] The Mt. Olive district, as well as the whole county, took pride in their good schools (Brewer, "History of Coosa County," 92).
[75] So far as is known, John W. Cotton had only one picture made. This one, a photograph, was made during the war with Dr. Andrew Hindsman. Years later Jefferson Davis Cotton had a picture of his father made from this and the "likness" of Dr. Hindsman was presumably destroyed by the photographer.

other letter he is not in our briggade I herd they were ordered back
here (tourn over) You rote that miss marten were coming here but
she ant come yet you said when I wanted any close I must let you no
I have sent to draw a shirt from the government they say we can draw
close in place of competition money[76] I dont think I will need any
more close til spring if you get a good chance you might send me a
shirt I could send you some money and if I thought you needed it I
would send it rite it if you need it and I well send it I have got $160
and we will draw $78 more in a few days we will be mustered today
for our pay if we have to take any more such marches as we have been
taking I will have to by me another horse for my horse is nearly wore
out our horses look very bad and there is but little chance to mend
them up here for we dont get nothing but corn and not enough of
that it is snowing little now this morning the first two days of march
were pretty weather dont bee uneasy about me for I can make out
anywhere anybody else can nothing more at present only I remain
your loving husband til death
John W Cotton to Mariah Cotton

Kingston Tennessee   february the 6   1863
Mariah Cotton Dear wife is again I take my pen in hand to rite you a
few lines to try to let you no that I am well and I hope these few lines
may reach you all the same we are not doing as well as we have been
we hant drawn any meat in several days we hant had any thing to eat
only as we bought it only rice and corn bread and the meal not sifted
there is a heap of complaint about something to eat for myself I can
make out to live where any body else can I recken we will get some
meat this evening if we dont we will have to kill a hog I hant got but
little to rite to you but asa is riting and I will send this with hisen he
is well and porter has come back to the company he is not very well
yet but a heap better we have one man in our company that is very
sick with pneumony the rest of the company is doing very well I would
like to come home and see how thing are doing and see you and the
children and bee with you all awhile I could tell you a heap I cant
rite to you I would like to see how manuel is getting on farming and
see to things in general I dont want you to bee uneasy about me atall
I will come home as soon as I can but I dont want you to look for
me atall when you rite again rite all the nuse let me no where bill is

[76] See earlier explanation.

and what he is doing and whether wash is at home or not tell wash to rite to me rite how miss holingshead is making out since mose has gone to the war bill brown hant got here yet we are looking for the captain and several men in a few days I hant herd from dock yet nor I hant herd from mike since he left here nothing more at present only I remain your true loving and affectionate husband til death

Kingston Tennessee February 7th 1863
Mariah dear wife it is once more that I take my pen in hand to rite a few more lines to let you no that I am well and doing well as common we have some very cold weather here now there is a big snow on the ground for two days and three nites it ant melted any hardly yet but this is a beautiful morning I hant but little to rite to you the first georgia regiment has left here and gone to rogersville 60 miles above knoxville and 2 companies of our regiment is ordered to greenville 65 miles above knoxville on the railroad to gard the town our company and captain rollens company they say we will start tomorrow I am afraid we wont get off there for I want to get away from our colonel none of our regiment hardly dont like him he is drunk ever time he can get the whiskey to get drunk on[77] there is 6 of our mess sent for a transfer to ashleys[78] company it is at polend below montgomery I think I will stay with the company a while longer I am getting along very well with it I would be very well satisfied if I could get a furlow to come home to see you all I think if we go to greenville I will get a furlow You must do the best you can til I get to come home I hope these few lines will find you and the children well and doing well I got the letter you sent by brady and one since dated the 23 of January I was very glad to here that you are well and doing so well you said the cows looked so bad I was sorry to here that but glad to here they had brought you 3 calves if they live threw the winter you will get milk a plenty tell the children I will come to see them some of these times we have just drawed 4 months wages I would be glad if you had some of my money for I have got more than I want to keep in camp I will send this letter by lieutenant Patridge to pinkneyville nothing more at present I remain your affectionate husband til death   John W. Cotton

[77] There was a great deal of complaint about drunken officers. There is no evidence here that any punishment was meted out to any officer but there was "An act to Punish Drunkeness in the Army" (*Statutes* II, 47 April 21, 1862) which provided that any commissioned officer who should be "found drunk on or off duty" should be either suspended or publicly reprimanded.
[78] Probably the company of Capt. W. P. M. Ashley, from Georgia.

Knoxville Tennessee   February the 11 1863
Mariah dear wife we are at knoxville or near there to stay all nite we
are on our march to greenville we have stoped here to draw some
amunition and mules bridals and rashions and so on   I hant but little
to rite to you these lines leaves me in fine health and I hope these few
lines may find you all in the same health our teem is not able to take
us to greenville and we will have to return them here and get better
mules to take us to greenville we are only allowed four mules to the
company and one wagon we only travil 12 or 15 miles a day   I am in
hopes we will stay at greenville Tennessee   It is 65 miles above knoxville on the railroad we are going there to gard a bridge we will leave
here tomarrow evening there is several of our men afoot and we get
along slowly but we have got our own time to go in our horses is very
low in order our trip to kentucky had like to have killed our horses I
have got about the best horse in our company there is no excitement
here now there is no expectation of a battle no where   I here of only
in virginery they are expecting the yankeys to make there last effort to
take richmond but from what I can here it will bee in vane   I hope
to god that the thing will soon end and I will get to come home to you
and my little ones dont get out of hart but bee of good cheer do the
best you can and I will come home as son as I can I think I will get a
furlow before long   Asa is well but william lessley is not well he is just
able to travel all of our company is well that is along to travel there is
several gone home on sick furlows   me and Asa will try to come home
together if we come atall but you need not look for us til you see us
I hope these few lines may find you all in fine sperits and doing well
nothing more at present I remain your affectionate husband til death
J. W. Cotton

February 12th 1863   Mariah I will rite you a few more lines this morning to let you no that I am well and hope these few lines may find you
all well some of our men come to us last that had started home a furlow without the generals name to it and they could not go on the railroad and they say the general here wont sine a furlow atall so I dont
recken I will get to come home without I runaway nothing more you
said you wanted me to send my weight   I waid yesterday evening I
waid one hundred and eighty two

Greenville Tennessee   February 20th. 1863
Dear wife it is with pleasure I rite you a few lines to let you no that I
am well I am still mending I waid this morning 185 pounds I hope

these few lines may find you all enjoying the same blessing we have got to greenville we got here last nite I rote to you while we were at knoxville we have had a bad trip from knoxville to greenville it rained on us a good deal and the roads were the muddiest that ever I seen it was one eternal mud hole and our mules gave out and we had to lay-over one day and put our things all on the railroad and put some of our horses to the wagons to get them here we will stay here some time I xpect as curiers I think there is a chance for us to stay here til spring I think we will do tolerable well if we can get feed for our horses we here forage is scarce I hant got much to rite porter was left at knox-ville sick he was rite sick when we left him I reckon he will get a sick furlow he may get home before you get this letter asa is well the health of the company is better than it has been in a good while we have got more men for duty than we have had in som time our horses looks very bad but if we could get forage a plenty we could mend them up greenville is a very pretty little town but they have got the small pox here but only a few of us will stay in town at a time the rest will stay about 20 miles from here where forage is more plenty when you rite again rite bill and wash what the conscript has done with them.

February the 21   Mariah I am still well I hope you all are the same we have got to go back to kingston today or start we got a order last nite to go back to kingston Tennessee nothing more at present I re-main your affectionate husband til death rite how you are getting on with your crop

John W Cotton

Kingston tennessee February 28th 1863
Dear wife and children it is with much pleasure that I take my pen in hand to let you no that I have just red two letters from you last nite one dated the 1 of the February and the other the 14 you said all were well except had coles I was glad to here that you were all well and you said you were doing very well and your stock were doing very well but your milk cows you ort to try to keep them alive til spring for milk cows wil be worth something butter is worth one dollar per pound and milk one dollar per gallon corn is from 3 to 5 dollars per bushel and meet according everything is very scarce ever where we go we got back from greenville last nite and we found things very scarce we had a rough trip of it but we done very well we had no tents after we left knoxville and when we left greenville we returned our

wagon and put our things on the cars and sent them back to kingston so we had to toat our provisions on our horses and get them cooked as we could our boys spent a site of money on the trip I werent out but little I made back what I spent but I done it honestly some of our men pressed horses and some sold horses and the squad now was reported at knoxville by the owners and it was stoped as we came threw there and the command was examine for the horses but none were found they had swoped most off and some of them were off from the command and they went around knoxville so they have all come clere so fare I saw William lessley as I came threw knoxville and he was a heap better than he was when we left him we herd when we were gone to greenville a rite smart about peace but I dont put no faith in nothing I here yet but a great many think that peace will soon bee maid I hope it will but I am afraid it will not come soon I want to come home the wourst you ever saw but I dont see much chance to come yet I have almost forgot how the children look I want to see how much they have growed I reckon Ann nearly grown when you rite let me no whether little ginney can walk or not and tell me all about the children is coming on rite all of the news and how manuel is getting on with his crop and how the wheat looks I cant think of half I want to rite it is raining and I hant got much to rite we hant got our tents yet but they are at the boat landing they will bee here this eavning we had the worst rain on us day before yesterday than we have since we have been in the service the river is up very hy our trip injured our horses a great deal some of them gave out and we left them we had to leave William Lessleys horse my horse is nearly wore out all of our horses look very bad I dont expect we will stay here very long nothing more at present only I remain your loving husband till death

John W. Cotton

Kingston Tennessee March the 13, 1863
Mariah Cotton Dear wife I take my pen in hand this morning to rite you a few lines to let you no that I am well and hope these few lines may reach you all enjoying the same blessing I hope you are all well and doing well I hant but little to rite to you only to let you no that I am well I think there is some chance now to get a furlow before long Colonel good is gone to knoxville and the officers says that he is going to try to get a order to furlow ten men out of company at a time till all of the men goes home that hant been home since we left montgomery if he gets that order I may get to come home some time this spring

but I dont want you to look for me for Colonel good may not get no order to gave furlows   Asa is well porter is better than he has been the company is in tolerable good health Captain Slaughter hant come back yet he started here and got to talladega town and got sick and went back they say he wont never come to us bill brown hant got here yet we are still getting more recruits we have sent off some of our horses to recruits them up we sent 25 horses from every company to tend to them I sent mine with them we sent them off about forty miles where they can get corn and hay plenty they say they will stay about two months I rote a letter to dock day before yesterday I hant herd from him since mike left here I hant hern from you in just a month the last letter I got was dated the 14 of february I want to here from you very bad I have looked and looked for a letter til I have got tired and hant got nary one yet I think the falt lies in the mail between home and montgomery I am afraid you ant a getting my letters neither I rite one every week and sometimes oftener I dont want you to bee uneasy about me for I am doing very well and could do better if I could keep from studying about home rite to me how manuel is getting on with his crop and how the wheat and rye and oats and stock looks and how the colt looks and how all the children is doing and how you are yourself nothing more John W. Cotton

Kingston Tennessee March the 17 1863
Mariah I have juste herd from you for the first time in over a month I was very glad to here from you all but sorry to here you all had such bad colds but I was glad that there was nothing worse the matter billy brown got here yesterday morning and brought me a letter I was glad to here that you were getting on so well with your crop and glad to here that everything was doing as well as what it was you said you had all of the children vaccinated but little ginney but you never said whether it hurt them much or not it is strange that it dident take on you I hant never been vaccinated yet there ant any danger here now of small pox Joe learnet saw John Tramel the other day and he said mike was very sick he said he thought mike had the dropsy I dont no but I expect he is gone home before now if he is able to go John was going down below here to a place called mouse creek to recruit up some of there horses and mules the rest of the sick ones is gone down there and all that was able to travel has gone to kentucky to mount them-selves you said you wanted to no if bud had got a transfer to Tramels company he hant got it but he could get it yet if would try there hant been any thing done about it since I rote about it but lieutenant beard

says he will grant him a transfer any time we are getting tolerable good
rashions now our meet is mostly new bacon we get rice flour meal and
bacon I want to come home very bad but there is no chance now we
got an order the other day to issue no furlows nor details so there will
be no chance til that order is countermanded you said you wanted to
no whether I wanted any close or not I will want some summer close
two pare of pants and one shirt I drawed a (   ) home spun shirt
last nite and the one you brought me last summer is a good shirt yet
but my checked shirts is wore out if you get the chance you may send
them to me but I hope I will get to come home before I need them
dont bee uneasy about me for I am doing very well and I dont think
there is any danger of our getting into a fite nothing more John W
Cotton to Mariah Cotton his wife

Kingston Tennessee March the 23 1863
Dear wife   I again attempt to rite you a few lines to let you no that
I am well all to a bad cold but I am better of it   Asa is well but
porter is very porely and Loney bullerd one of our mess has been rite
sick but he is a heap better there is some more of the boys complaining
but not very bad off   I begin to here from you very bad again brown
brought me a letter when he come that is all the letter I have got since
the 11th of february it looks like the mail has stopped we here that
they are going to stop it from wetumpka to taladega if you get this rite
in your next letter whether you get my letter or not I rite one every
weak to you I think I will rite today to John and rachael[79] for the
first time since I left montgomery I hant got mutch to rite to you we
have moved from where we have been camped to the opposite side of
town about two miles from where we were but closter to town the hole
regiment is campted in a square and we have a gard round the hole
regiment we have a heap more gard duty to do now than we ever have
had and titer rules but they ant two tite yet for some of the men has
been doing all of the duty and others none I think I rote to you about
hereing that mikes beeing sick and John W Trammel said he thought
he has the dropsy   John is at mouse creek recruiting some horses and
mules   I think I will rite to him and try to here from mike   I rote to
dock not long ago but I hant got no answer from him yet you dont no
how bad I want to here from you all and I want to see you a hap worse
but there ant no chance to come to see you now if I could see you I
could tell you a heap that I cant think of to rite and if could think of

79 John W. Fulmer was married to his sister Rachel.

it would take me too long to rite it all I cant come to see you without running away and I dont want to do that for when men runs away and comes back they put some of them in jail and I dont want to go there for I hant been crossed nor on double duty since I have been in the war nor I hant had a cross word with my officers nothing more only I remain your loving husband till death John W Cotton
I will send you some seed called pie melons plant them like a water melon

Kingston Tennessee March the 27. 1863
Dear wife it is with pleasure that I again have the opportunity to answer your kind letter which I received yesterday morning I was glad to here that the children were all well but sorry to here that you had such a bad cold and cough but I hop when these few lines reaches you you will bee well I was sorry to here that you had lost one of your cows but them has must loose[80] this is the first letter that I have received from you since the 14 of february this is dated the 15 of march I got a few lines from Porter verdamon he said he wanted to borrow my led pipeing and take my iron and make my boiler for the use of it til I come home if he comes after it let hime have them he can take them and make the boiler and if he wares it out he can pay me the iron back it wont hurt the pipeing I will rite to him about it I was glad to here that your grain looks so well I hope there will bee a good crope of grain made this year wheat up here looks very well you said you was afraid you would have your bacon pressed from you[81] I dont think it would bee rite for them to press a pore mans propery and him in the war I dont no what to tell you to do I herd yesterday that bacon was worth $1.25 cents per pound in montgomery I think if you could get that you had better hire somebody to hall it down there and sell it then to have it pressed at 60 cents per pound it looks like as you are home and me here in the war and so many little children to support that you ort to have as much for anything you have to sell as any body else if times dont get no better I think bacon will be one dollar and a half or two dollars per pound it selling up here from

---

80 Some more of his rural folk philosophy.
81 No one liked impressment of provisions but it seemed the most sensible plan for getting supplies for the army. Impressment had been going on since 1862 but a new law had been passed the day before this letter had been written. Schedules of prices were to be published every two months and were always lower than current prices. (Fleming, *Civil War and Reconstruction* 174-175; *Public Laws,* 1st Congress, 3rd session, March 26, 1863).

forty to fifty cts per pound eggs fifty cts a dozen butter $1.00 per pound and we cant hardly get any at that whickey is worth from 4 to 5 dollars a qt in the cuntry and ten dollars per quart in camps and one dollar per drink billy brown is gone out today after some I went out the other day and me and bunter shaw and got some and got water bound and had to stay all nite and then had to swim our horses across a big creek next morning I sold what I got and made about forty dollars I went out one day before and made about twenty five dollars on some there is a heap of specalating in camps on whiskey[82] if I could see you I could tell you a heap more than I can rite it would bee a heap of satisfaction to me to come home once more and see you all tell ann to bee a smart girl and lern fast tell bud and bunk to bee smart boys and help manuel mowin corn to keep the pigs fat tell all of the children I want to see them tel babe and sweet I will bring them some candy when I come home nothing more at present only I remain you true affectionate husband til death these few lines leaves me well dont bee uneasy about me John W. Cotton

Kingston Tennessee Aprile the 1. 1863
Dear beloved wife I again take my pen in hand to rite you a few lines in answer to your kind letter which I red dated march the 20 I red it with great satisfaction I was glad to here that you were all well and doing well as what you was I was glad to here that manuel was getting on with his crop as well as he was and glad to here that every thing was doing well we are doing tolerable well here now we get corn bread and new bacon but we have a heap of duty to do we have to stand camp guard and provose guard and picket guard and then there is most always some of us on the scout some of our boys went out on a scout last weak and brought in a man supposed to bee a bushwhacker and colonel good turned him loose and some of us men went with him and when they had got him about a half of a mild a cross the river they tride to hang him and they could not get him hy enough off of the ground to choke him to death and they shot him twice and left him hanging there and the colonel found it and had six of them arrested and put in jail but I dont no what he will do with them if I could see you I could tell you a heap more about it but I recken this is enough our colonel is getting titer every day he has got

82 Much speculation went on among the troops (John Christopher Schwab, *The Confederate States of America,* New York: Scribners, 1901, chapter XI, E. Merton Coulter, *The Confederate States of America,* chapter XI).

30 or 40 in jail some for one thing and some for another he had two taken this morning for deserting there post last nite the hole regiment I think would be glad if he was dead he speaks of going to kentucky in ten or twelve days but I dont think we will go that soon I think we will stay here a good while or somebody will have to stay here you rote to me about vardamans comeing after my still[83] arrangements if he comes after them let him have them you rote about your money you said if I owed any thing you could pay it if I owe any thing I dont no it[84] you said you wanted to use it in some way I don't no how you will use it unless you buy land or negroes if you get enough buy you a waiter girl[85] I have money enough here to do me a while I have got $245 I herd from my horse the other day they say he was mending adkins is tending to him we have had some very bad weather here for a few days it snowed yesterday evening and last night and the wind bleau very hard and there was ice here this morning more than a half an inch thick but the weather is moderating very fast there ant nobody here planting any corn yet wheat looks very well but late we have drawn 8 days rashons since I begun this letter we draw 6 day rashons of corn meal 2 of flour new bacon rice pees vinegar and soap and salt we have got sixty six in camp and 7 with our horses Mr. brown says he is getting very home sick the body lice[86] bothers him very bad you ort to see him rakeing and scratching and cracking them porter is some better asa is well we have got 2 men at the horsepitol very sick it ant worth while to try to write all to you that I could tell you if I could see you these few lines leaves me well and doing well I hope when you come to reed them you may bee enjoying the same nothing more at present only I remain your loving and affectionate husband til death to His wife and family John W. Cotton

Kingston Tennessee Aprile the 3 1863
dear wife I have not started my letter yet I gave it to a nin caho to mail at taladega but he did not start home according to promise so I will now send it by mail I received your kind letter last nite dated

---

83 This is the first of many references to his still.

84 In all the Coosa County records there is no instance of a mortgage or any other recorded debt.

85 His interest in buying a slave in 1863 can be understood but he keeps on talking about it even after he admits the war is lost for the Confederacy. Even in the last letter (February 1, 1865) he writes his wife he could get a negro if he had some way of sending her home.

86 Body lice caused great discomfort to Confederates. See Wiley, *Johnny Reb*, 250-251.

march the 24 I was glad to here from you and to here that you all are
well and doing well these lines leave me well and doing well you rote
that you could not help being uneasy about me you need not uneasy
yourself about me still for I am doing as well as any body can in
camps I was glad to here miss holingshead was doing so well and glad
to here that mose stood camps as well as he does I am glad wash[87] is
at home yet you said that carline had not herd from bill[88] but you
never said where caroline was at you never rite nothing about tony[89]
rite in your next letter if you here from him you said you herd the
government was pressing bacon here they are pressing bacon but they
are pressing beef cattle it ant no use to say anything about comeing
home but you may rest assured that I will come as soon as I get the
chance nothing more at present only I remain your true belov husband
til death   John W Cotton

Kingston Tennessee April 11th 1863
Dear wife I take my pen in hand to answer your kind letter which I
received yesterday it was a letter I recon you aimed to send by nan gray
but capt Slaughter brought it it had a plat of your hair[90] in it that
looked very natural but I had a heap rather seen you but I was glad
to here that you were well and doing well I hant got but lettle to rite
only to let you no that I am well and doing well we have a plenty to
eat now and a plenty to do we are on duty about every other day there
is one hundred and twenty of our men gone on a 15 days scout and
we started 7 men yesterday morning with a disptach to montevallo[91]
general pegrims briggade went to Kentucky and met the yankeys and
got a whipping and had to fall back[92] John Tramels company is in the
briggade but he was not with them. he was left not far from here
with some horses and mules to fatten up and Mike wernt with them

87 Wash Smith who married Mary Ann Cotton on May 11, 1843 (*Marriage Records,* Coweta County).
88 He had a brother William so this may be he since he is naming kinfolk.
89 Tony Pate was the second husband of Sarah Cotton; her first marriage to
Joseph B. Pitts, May 21, 1850 (Marriage Records, Coweta County) was unhappy
and of short duration. (Mrs. Nannie Cotton, June 10, 1950) Sarah and Tony Pate
are buried in Mt. Pleasant cemetery.
90 This, or a similar plat, is still in the family Bible. It is medium brown and
several inches long.
91 This could be Montevallo, Alabama or Monticello, Kentucky.
92 General John Pegram's brigade was on detached service from January 20 to
April 1, 1863 (*The War of the Rebellion: A compilation of the Official Records of
the Union and Confederate Armies,* Washington: Government Printing Office, 1889,
Series I Vol. XXIII, p. 746 [Cited hereafter as *Official Records*]).

neither for he was sick when they started to kentucky and I hant herd
from him yet I rote about his beeing sick before Asa is off a carrier
from here to knoxville he stays 9 miles from here 1 in about a weak he
will be back tonite or tomorrow my horse is at the convelessent camps
yet the horses that is here gets a plenty to eat now our colonel is getting very tite on us he gets titer and titer every day he has got lots of
the boys under arrest now and some for very small crimes you said you
wanted me to tell you what to do with your money I dont no what to
tell you if you can lend it out and get good notes for it it would be
best thing you could do but I dont reckon there is any body that wants
to borrow if you cant lend it if you can find anything you want you
can by it I wish I could come home and stay a few days til I could see
how things were going on but I had rather come to stay but there is
no chance to get a furlow now there ant nobody getting furlows but
the officers I dont want you to bee uneasy about me I could do very
well if I could keep from studying about home it ant worth while for
me to try to tell you how much I study about home but there is one
thing that gives me great consolation you have a plenty to live upon
and from what I lern there is lots of soldiers wives that has not much
to eat if I were to here that you had nothing to eat I should come
home at the risk of my life[93] you rote a rite smart about the children
tell them I want to see them and I will come to see them as soon as I
can you may send them to school if you can do without them but I
no you are lonesome enough without sending them off I wish you had
somebody to stay with you I will send you a song ballet that soots the
times[94] very well nothing more at present only I remain your true
devoted husband til death   John W Cotton

[93] Dr. Martin says the chief cause of desertions was poverty in the families of the
soldiers (Bessie Martin, *Desertion of Alabama Troops from the Confederate Army,*
New York; Columbia University Press, 1932, p. 127-135). See also Ella Lonn,
Desertion During the Civil War, New York: The Century Company, 134. Coosa
County, while it was not considered one of the wealthy counties, had a small per-
centage (27%) of indigent families and did not receive state aid until 1864 (Martin, *op. cit.* 130). Coosa County, however, settled a sum of money on families
earlier. The basis for these appropriations is difficult to discover but it was not
always poverty. On August 12, 1862, the family of J. W. Cotton composed of eight
members, was granted $200, Asa Waldrop's family of five was given $500 and A. C.
L. Hindsman's of one, $75 (Minutes of Commissioner's Court, Coosa, County)
Book 8, 321-326). Later it was found that some families needed more and addi-
tional sums were given them but the Cottons were not included.
[94] Unfortunately this "ballet" is not with the letters.

Kingston Tennessee April 16th 1863

Dear beloved wife it is again I take my pen in hand to answer your
kind letter which I received a few days ago I would have rote sooner
but I had just rote when I got your letter I was glad to here that you
were all well and doing as well as what you were I was glad to here
that manuel was getting along so well with his crop I hope he will be
attentive to his business and made you a good crop I hant got but
very little to rite only to let you no that I am well and doing well
but there is a heap of our men getting sick floid goodgame is very
sick we have got orders to move from here out about one mile east of
town we are going to move on account of health the doctors think it
will be healthyer to move our colonel is getting titer and titer there
ant but too privates allowed to leave a company at a time and one
officer and he only can bee gone two hours at a time Captain slaughter
is with us now but some think he wont stay long nearly all of our men
is in camps now but there is no furlowing agoing on and I dont see
much chance to come home at all but dont get out of hart I will do
all I can to get to come home it may come to my time after while
Asa is still a curier he stays 9 miles from here he was here last nite he
was well porter is in better health now than he has been since he come
back from kentuckey but he is not well yet hant come back to our
company yet I am looking for a letter from him now I hant herd
nothing from him since I rote about him an I hant herd nothing from
Mike nor John my horse is at the convalessent camp yet they say
he is mending I here they are expecting a fight at murfeysborough in
a few days I here of several fights here lately and our men has got the
best of it on nearly all of them the report of general pegrims getting
such a whipping is disputed insted of his beeing whiped back he has
gone on to lancaster kentucky and had another fite and whiped the
yankeys there that is 20 miles from lexington it ant worth while to
rite anthing about the war for you will here it by the papers[95] before I
can rite it to you I want you to rite all the nuse when you rite I got
your letters more regular now than I ever have since I left mongomery
I will send a letter that I got from John Fulmer if you hant had
little crickets funeral preached yet dont have it preached til I come

[95] We do not know, of course, what papers the Cottons read. The latest check
list (Rhoda Ellison, *A Check List of Alabama Imprints* 1807-1870, University of
Alabama Press, 1946) names the Wetumpka *Argus* and Wetumpka *Dispatch* as
county papers of the period. It may have been the Montgomery *Advertiser* or,
since their ties with Georgia were so close, a paper from that state.

home[96] if ever I come that is one thing that I hate to rite about or talk about I cant hardly rite or talk about her without shedding tears I never shal forget how she use to fondle on my knees and her antic motions and her little prattling tongue but all this is past and she is at rest and is better off than her bereaved parents nothing more at present only I remain your affectionate husband til death

John W. Cotton

Kingston Tennessee Aprile the 22 1863
Dear beloved wife it is again that I take my pen in hand to answer another kind letter that I received from you a few days ago I was very glad to here that the children was well but sorry to here that you had such a bad cold and such a horceness I shal bee uneasy until I here from you again I am afraid it will run into the phneumonia these lines leaves me well and doing tolerable well and I hope when you come to reed them you will bee well and doing well and all of the rest of you we have a heap of duty to do yet and colone good herd the other day that the yankeys had flanked general pegrim at cumberlan river and were makeing there way to kingston and so last friday morning we got orders to bee ready to march to meet them with too days rashons cooked and we our meat to draw so we fixed up as soon as possible and started the horsemen went a head and the footmen after them of which I were one for my horse were at the convalessent camp with two hundred and fifty others but the colonel sent after our horses for them to bee brought to camp and if we needed them for them to bee brought to us and he had one hundred and twenty men out on a scout he sent for them too we went about 10 miles the first day and the cavalry went in about twenty miles and camped close to a little town and Colonel good and several more of the officers went to town that nite and got drunk and we went on 7 or 8 miles next morning and met them comeing back and they said they could not here of any yankeys so we all turned around and started back for

---

[96] The deferred funeral was popular by rural necessity. Literature available confines the custom to the mountain sections but the practice continued in many sections well into the twentieth century. The editor of these letters, as a child, attended one where, on a Sunday afternoon, the funeral of a man's wife was preached with great feeling. The bereaved sat alone on the front bench, weeping copiously although the departed had been dead more than a year and he had re-married. The new wife was obligingly absent. Two sources of the delayed funeral are John C. Campbell, *The Southern Highlander and His Homeland,* New York: Russell Sage Foundation (1921) p. 148-150, and Jean Thomas, *Blue Ridge Country,* New York: Duell, Sloan and Pearce (1942) p. 155-158.

camps the cavalry got back that nite and we got back where we got
the first nite and stayed all nite and come back to camp next morning
there was a heap of our infantry give out and fell behind but they got
in that day I stood it tolerable well but I got very tired of it my feet
and legs got very sore but I have got about over it now our officers and
men did not like the way our colonel managed our trip they say there
was no use for the infantry to go our colonel is very much disliked
by the regiment I dont think you see much satisfaction from the way
you rite you said you had not been to meeting[97] since I left home nor
where else only where you had business I would bee much better
satisfyed if I new you were enjoying your self by going to see your
neighbours and to meeting and so on I think if you would go about
more you would enjoy your self better than you do I try to pass off
the time the best I can but I cant keep from studying about home it
would gratify me more now to come home than anything you could
mention and there ant nothing to hinder us from comeing only con-
trariness in our officers you said you wanted me to tell you what to do
with your money I dont no what to tell you only to do the best you
can you spoke of thread beeing $15 per bunch I think you had better
buy cloth than to pay that much for thread if you can get such as
soots you as for my close I shall soon need some pants but our captain
says he is going to try to detail some men to go after our summer
close nothing more at present only I remain your true affectionate
husband till death John W Cotton

Kingston Tennessee   Aprile the 27. 1863   Dear beloved wife it is with
pleasure that I take my pen in hand to rite you a few lines in answer
to your kind letter which I red last nite   I was glad to here you were
all well and doing well and I was glad to her that you did not like
any thing but me   you said you thought if you me at home you would
be hapy   I would bee hapy to come if it was only for a few days but I
had much rather come to stay all the time   I was glad to here that
manuel was getting along so well with his crop and I hope from what
you say you will make a good crop of small grain   I would bee glad if
I could bee at to help cut it but if I do it be only a happenso for there
is not much furlowing agoing on and if any body were to get furlows
it would bee men that are sick and complaining I am always able for

---

[97] It may have been expected that religion would be important in the lives of
this family. There is no note of irreligion, and while a high moral tone runs
through the letters, there are very few references to the church and requests for
prayer for his safety are largely confined to times of hard fighting.

duty and they wont furlow such men if they can help it   these lines leave me well and I hope that when you come to reed this short letter you may bee enjoying the same blessing   I got the ring and sweet gum you sent to me   I would not take nothing for it   you said you made it a Sunday   you ort not work a sunday but go to meeting and to see your neighbors but we poor devils have to work a sunday as well as any other day but I will send you a ring of my own make and see how you like it   I couldev made it nicer if I had have had the rite sort of tools you rote about the children tell them all that I want to see them tell them they must bee smart children   it ant worth while for me to try to say any thing about how bad I want to see you all   I would like to see babe with his breeches on and see his capers and see little giney runabout and play but I have no idea she would no me if she were to see me tell sweet he must lern to talk before I come home tell bud and bunk they must help manuel cut bushes and weeds and make a heap of corn tell ann she must bee a good girl and lern a heap and bee kind to her teacher and lern to rite   billy brown is sick he is at the horse-pitol he look tolerable bad   it is cold that ailds him there is a heap of our company sick and complaining   floid goodgame is very bad off yet   porter is better off now than he has been since he come back from kentucky   Asa is well and so is all of our mess   our horses is at the convalessent camps yet and I expect adkins has sold my horse he said he could get $80 for him and I told him to sell him ant no account I will have to by me another horse any how porter[98] has got to by him a horse too there is a heap of the boys a foot and there ant no horses about here to buy and they are hyer than ever   I saw horses and every thing else is hyere than ever I saw   it look like men dont care any thing about money   we bought two old hens this morning and paid two dollars for them and butter is worth one dollar per pound and eggs the same per dosen nothing more at present only I remain your dear beloved husband til death John W. Cotton

Kingston Tennessee   May the 1 1863

Dear beloved wife it is with pleasure that I take my pen in hand to answer your kind and affectionate letter which I red late nite with pleasure dated april the 20 I was very glad to here that you were all well but bunk I was sorry to here that he had such a sore foot I was sorry to here that you had not got nary letter from me in ten days for I no you want to here from me as often as you can I would bee

---

[98] Porter, although he is mentioned frequently, remains unidentified.

glad to here from you every day I rite you a letter to you every weak
and some times oftener I wish I could get out letters sooner than I do
for it almost always takes a letter 10 or 12 days to come to me you
spoke of every thing being so hy every thing is very hy here and are
still useing horses it looks like is clere out of reason there cant bee a
horse bought here that is fit to ride for less than 250 or 300 dollars
and I have got to have one for my horse want never bee no more account but if I get the chance I will raise me a horse from some of these
old linconites about here but I will have to wait til we go to leave here
or take it off and trade it I have got money enough to by a horse or
will have in a few days but I dont want to spend it in that way we will
draw two months wages in a few days we were mustered yesterday for
our pay they will pay us up to the first of may I havent got but very
lettle to rite at the present but if I was with you so I could tell you
things as I could think of them I could tell you heaps of ups and
downs that is two tedious to rite here we are expecting a fite at tula-
homer[99] they are having skermish fighting there every day but no
regular ingagements our men have stayed here till they are getting
very ressless they are very anxious to go home and anxious for the
war to end a heap of them says there fameleys is out of provisions and
they cant by it with the money and they assign a heap of reasons for
wanting it to end a heap of them talks of going home but very few
of them goes I want to come home as bad as any body can it looks to
me like but I shant run away yet maby I will get a furlow some time
or other I dont want it throwed up to my children after I am dead
and gone that I was a deserter from the confederate army I dont want
to do anything if I no it that will leave a stain on my posterity hereafter I was glad to here that your crop looked so well and manuel was
getting on so well with his crop nothing more at present only I remain your kind and affectionate husband til death   John W. Cotton

Kingston Tennessee May the 5. 1863 My dear beloved wife it is with
much pleasure that I take my pen in hand to rite you a few lines to
answer your kind letter which I received dated the 24 of Aprile I was
glad to here that you were all well but bunk I was sorry to here that
he was having such bad boils I am in hopes when I here from home

[99] The headquarters of the Army of Tennessee were at Tullahoma. Correspondence about these activities can be found in *Official Records*, series I vol. XXIII.
Horn (*The Army of Tennessee*) says that no other Confederate Army "enjoyed
such a protracted period of inaction as the Army of Tennessee" during the first
half of 1863, p. 231. He seems to blame Bragg for the lack of action.

he will bee better and all the rest of you well these few lines leave me
well and doing very well I hant but little to rite at the present geneals
pegrims briggade has come out of kentucky they had another fite with
the yankeys and whiped them and when they got them a running they
tuck up a retreat for tennessee they say they left the yankeys 6 miles
this side of Montacello you said you was in hopes you would make
some wheat if the rust did not kill it I am in hopes you will make a
good crop of small grain and corn too and I hope I will get home to
help gather corn but I am afraid not there is more men wanting the
war to end than ever I saw they are all getting tired of it if the big
officers were as tired of it as the pore privates it would soon end but
I am afraid they will carry it on a heap longer the papers speak a rite
smart about fighting but I cant think there will be as hard fiting as
has been the yankeys are tired of it as well as we are I think we will
stay here a good while if the yankeys dont run us off from here and I
dont think there is much danger of that I am in hopes that if there
ant much fiting done before the water falls and the rivers gets two lo
the gun boats to run there wont much more done at all for I am in
hopes they will come in come terms of peace this summer I would
give a rite smart for them to make peace you dont no how much good
it would do me to start home to stay it would do me a heap of good to
start home for a few days but if I had no ties at home I would as
leave stay here as any where nearby I should not like to be under such
close confinement we dont have as mauch gard duty to do now as we
have had we dont have no camp gard now we are seeing tolerable
easy times but we have more gard duty to do than necessary. lieutenant beard is trying to get a detail to come home after horses I would
like to come but I dont expect I shal there is so many that hant got
horses at all and I have got a thing but he wont never be able for duty
any more I told bill adkins to sell him or swop him if they come home
after horses dont expect they can get them there ant no chance to get
them here without pressing them nothing more at present only I remain your true devoted friend til death John W Cotton to Mariah
Cotton

John W. Cotton to his wife and children

Kingston Tennessee   May the 7 1863   Dear wife it is again that I
take my pen in hand to rite you a few lines to let you no that we are
going to leave here tomorrow morning at 7 oclock we are going to join
pegrims command at clinton[100] 28 miles from here we will leave our
tents here we have sent them to town we will have this time to stay I
think you may still send your letters here til you here from me again
they will bee sent from here to me I will rite as soon as I get to where
we stop these lines leave me well and I hope these few lines may find
you all the same I was in hopes a few days ago that I would get to
come home before long but thes move nocked it in the head so I dont
have any idea when I will get the chance to come to see you all dont
get out of hart for I will come as soon as I can dont bee uneasy about
me I will bee shure to take care of myself take care of your self and our
little children and dont work yourself to death but enjoy yourself the
best you can I am in hopes I will get a letter from you to nite our
horses will bee here to nite from the convalessent camps we have got
everything ready to start in the morning nothing more at present only
I remain your trues devoted husband til death   John W Cotton

Monticello Kentucky May the 14 1863
Dear beloved wife it is with much pleasure that I take my pen in hand
to ancer your kind letter which I received since I left kingston   I am
glad to here from you all one time more and to here that you are well
and doing well these lines leave me well and doing well I rote you
that we were going to clinton   we went clinton but we only stayed
there one nite and then we started to kentucky we are now camped
near Monticello   we are now in the enemys land the yankeys are
not fare from us I dont no how clost   I expect we will bee in a battle
be fore many days there is a good many troops comeing in here they are
going to try the same yankeys that whiped general pegrim and if they
dont look sharp we will worst them   we have come here to whip them
general morgan whiped some of them last Sunday and ran them across
the cumberland river they fought in about 15 miles from here I dont
no how long we will stay here we may leave here to nite and we may
stay here several days but I dont think we will stay here long we have
only stoped today to rest our horses and get something for them to eat
we travelled 5 days on three handfuls of corn only what little pastures
we could get but we are where we can get plenty for our horses and

ourselves too I will send this letter back to kingston tomorrow by some
currier this may bee the last one that I will get to send to you til we
get out of kentucky you may still direct your letters to kingston I can
get them from there if I can get from anywhere I am glad to think you
are doing well I think you will do (well) to make a living and if I
never come back home I want you to rase the children rite and do the
best you can yourself I hant got much idea but what I will come home
to see you all again but I dont no what mite hapen to me but I dont
fear the enemy I come out to fite and I am as ready as I ever will be
nothing more at the present only I remain your true devoted husband
til death

John W. Cotton

the
May 20. 1863

Kentucky camps near Monticello Mariah dear wife it once more that
I have the opportunity of riting you a few lines to let you no that I
am well and doing well I hope these few lines may find you all well
and doing well I hant herd from you since I rote before but I am
looking for a curier here with our mail I hope I will get a letter from
you I hant got much to rite to you but if I could see you I could tell
you a heap that has happened since we left kingston the boys are
mounting themselves very fast on good horses some they swop for and
some of them take them where ever they find them some of them has
to give up and some dont I hant got nary one yet but I intend to have
one before I come back out of kentucky there ant no danger of a fite
yet every thing is still the yankeys are all in the other side of the cumberland river I herd this morning that some of our armey had gone to
the river to cross that is fiftee miles from here I think there will bee a
move in a few days all of our men that were a foot is with a briggade
of infantry asa ant with us he is left at kingston as a currier there ant
no use talking about comeing home now but if I live to get back out of
kentucky I think I will come home dont bee uneasy about me for I ant
in any danger yet you may still rite to kingston they say they are going
to try to get the mail every weak a curier leaves here now directly to
take our letters to kingston nothing more at present only I remain
your true devoted husband til death John W Cotton   I want to see
you all very bad

Kentucky Camps 15 Miles from Monticello   May the 26 1863
Dear beloved wife it is with much pleasure that I rite you a few lines
in answer to your kind letter which I received yesterday and day before our carriers brought our mail from kingston and I got two letters
one dated the 9 one the 13 I was truely glad to here from you all and
very glad to here that you all were well and getting along so well I
am well and doing very well and hope when these lines come to hand
you will bee the same porter is well asa is not here he is still at kingston all of our company is well that is here there is a good many left at
kingston we have moved our camps about ten miles from where we
were on the account of gettin more handy to forage we dont get nere
enough for our horses forage is very scarce here it is a very broken
mountaineous cuntry and there ant much mud here it is the worst
kind of a bushwhacking cuntry but they dont fire on us they are
afraid of us all of the men has left the cuntry the yankeys are all on
the other side of cumbertant river 15 miles from here I dont think
there is any danger of a fite here some of our regiment has been standing picket there at the river them on one side and the yankeys on the
other and they mad and agreement not to shoot at each other and
some of our men went over among them and traded with them some
of them say they are very tired of the war and want to go home they
say a heap of there mens time is nearly out and when there time is out
they will go home and stay there I am getting very anious to cross the
river among the yankeys and so is a heap of our men[101] I hant got me
nary horse yet but my oald horse would do a rite smart of service yet
if he could get a plenty to eat I think if I could cross the river I could
get a horse from the yankeys that would not cost me nothing I aim to
get another before I leave kentucky any how there is lots of the boys
got horses since we come up here Captain slaughter has resigned and
gone home and we had another election for lieutenant I run against
our orderly sergent and got beat[102] and we elected william lessley for
our orderly sergeant I am glad to here that she[103] was lerning so fast
tell her she must lern all she can and bee a goo girl tell all the children I want to see them and I ould bee glad to see you if I am not

[101] One of the things that plagued the officials was fraternizing with the enemy.
It seems to have been an unwritten code that pickets did not fire on each other
(Coulter, *Confederate States*, 460-461, Wiley, *Johnny Reb*, 315-319).
[102] See above, October 21, 1862.
[103] This must be Ann, for she is the only one he has mentioned specifically in
connection with learning.

mistaken and I dont think I am I need not try to tell you any thing about when I will come home for I thought I would have been there before now you said you wanted me to rite what sort of close I wanted if you get the chance you may send me 2 shirts and 2 pare pants I wish my yarn shirts were at home I hate to tote them so much I hant got nary letter from dock but I herd he was a comeing to the company soon I ex pect that he is at our oald camp with the rest of the boys well I reckon this letter will start tomorrow nothing more at present only I remain your true de voted husband til death think of me when fare away for I may bee nearer in a comeing day   John W. Cotton

May the 28 1863   I am still well and hope you are the same my letter never started when I thought it would but they say it will start in the morning I am looking for the mail tonite I hope I will here from you all once more and here that you all are well regiment
I will send you a ring

May the 30 1863   Mariah my letter ant started yet but they say it will start to day we was ordered to Monticello nite before last at midnite to meet the enemy and our cariers did not start we went on in a mild of Monticello and we got orders to return to camps you out to have been here to have herd the boys curse they wanted to go on they said it was a misunderstanding betwixt two generals[104] that we were ordered out we herd that the yankeys was crossing the river by thousands but it was all false if I only could see you I could tell you a heap I am well   I am well

June the 3 1863
Kentucky camps near Montacello
Dear wife it is with much pleasure that I rite you a few lines to try to let you no that I am well and hope these few lines may find you all enjoying the same blessing I hant got much to rite to you nor much time to rite there is a man agoing hom out of the regiment and he will leave in a little while there is some prospect of a battle we had orders this morning to saddle before lite and bee ready in five minutes to leave we went about two miles and formed a line of battle and stayed there about 3 hours and we were ordered back to camps we got a dispatch that the yankeys were crossing the river but we found out it was a mistake they say we will leave kentucky in a short time we are briggaded under Scott[105] and it is forming at lanores

104 *Official Records*, Series I, vol. XXIII.
105 This was Col. John S. Scott (*Official Records*, Series I, XXIII, 793).

11121314151617181920

station not fare from knoxville it is thought when we get with the briggade we will be sent to north alabama when I get back to tennessee am a going to try to come home   I want to see you and our loved ones I dont want you to bee uneasy about me for I am a getting along very well nothing more at present only I remain your true devoted husband til death

John W. Cotton

pray for me when I am gone that I may safe return   I got a letter from you last sunday and was glad to here that you were well and doing well and glad to here that your wheat looked like it would make something and was glad manuel was getting on well with his crop.

Kentucky camp near Montacello June the 13. 1863
Mariah Dear wife it is again that I take my pen in hand to rite you a few lines in ancer to your kind letter which I received dated the 26 of may I was glad to here that you were all well and doing well and glad that you were likely to make a good wheat crop for I reckon it is very much needed I think a good wheat crop will help us out a heap wheat is very good up here everywhere we have been but it is very late here there is some that hant droped the bloom yet and some nearly ripe you said that it is dry when you rote I am in hopes that you had rain a plenty before long and will continue to get plenty til crops are made I hant much to rite to you but I reckon it will bee of a great importance to you these lines leave me well and harty well Mariah I am hapy to say to you that we have been into a battle[106] and all of our company came out safe I cam out untouched there was but two of our regiment killed and some few wounded but none mortal the fite commenced soon in the morning the yankeys came across the river in the nite and had like to have got on us before we new it we met them about a mild from our camp with about two hundred of our men they had fore regiments and were thrown in the line of battle when we attacted them we were run rite up on top of a ridg in about one hundred and twenty five yards of them and them a fireing on us we fell back a short distance and formed a line of battle and them fireing at us all the time we dismounted and made a charge on them and gave them a fire but they put it to us so that we were obliged to fall back so we kept falling back and fiting them for about two hours

106 The battle at Monticello, Ky. was on June 9 (*Official Records*, Series I, XXIII).

and a half and we could not get any reinforcements and beeing under a heavy fire all the time and them trying to out flank us we had to retreat back where we got reinforcements we fell back about 7 miles from where the fite commenced they follered us 5 miles and turned back we sent three regiments back after them and they overtook them rite where the fite tuck place in the morning and a heavy fite commenced and our men whiped them badly from then til nite and drove them back to the river and they crossed the river back that nite they got reinforcements of twelve hundred men but they did not get over in time to do them any good we did not fite them any in the evening they had two canon a shooting at us all the time as many of them as there was in the morning we killed more of them than they did of us[107] there loss during the day is about fifty and our fore kiled the first georgia was in the fite in the eavning and they never lost nary man we are looking for another fite every day but we are better prepared than we were before we have fore regiments rite here and two batterys and some more not fare off if they come back they will get hurt if they dont bring more help I saw mike about a week ago he had been sick but was getting about again there regiment is camped not fur from us but I hant had the chance to go to see them they were all well phelix and steve boswell and frank worthen were with mike when I saw him June 16 Mariah I hant sent off this letter yet I hant had the chance the mail hant left yet we have fell back 30 miles from Montacello we fell back a sunday it was thought the yankeys would follow but they hant yet nor I dont think they will we may go back in a few days and we may go to kingston it is not nown yet I saw mike yesterday morning he was complaining some but not much these lines leave me well and doing well and I hope they may reach you the same they ant no danger of a fite now nothing more at present I remain you forever John W. Cotton

June the 17 1863?   Mariah I hant sent off my letter yet I think I will start in the morning by a curier. I hant had nary letter from you in some time but I look for one by the next mail I want to here from you all very much and I want to come home very bad and I think I will come home when I get back to kingston if they dont give me a furlow I will come without one but I think there will be a chance for a furlow we are now at Jamestown tennessee   we come here yes-

---

[107] Brewer (*Alabama*, 693) says the Tenth Confederate Regiment at Monticello lost 8 killed, 19 wounded and 62 captured.

terday evening   I think we will leave here tomorrow for kingston or
lanores Station to join our briggade it is thought that we will go from
there to Mississippi or louseanna I dont think we will go back to
montacello any more every thing is in such an uprore that I dont
hardly no what to rite I recken you will think strange of the writing
on the other side of this letter it is a peace of paper[108] I picked up in
the clerks office in this place the court house has been broke open and
all of the papers in the clerks office is distroyed I picked up enough
paper to rite several letters on that is rote on one side we cant get any
paper till we get back to kingston I would like to bee at home to see
how your crop looks and see how manuel is getting on but I had
rather see you and the children than your crop nothing more rite all
the nuse in your next letter these lines leave me well and remaining
your true devoted husband til death fare well til I rite to you again
John W. Cotton

[Spring 1863?]
Mariah you must make manuel plant that field belou the house and
the one leach of the oveherd and as much of the newground as he
can tend have it broke up as soon as possible and if he has time make
him fill up the cross fence between the oald field and pave I will send
this by lieutenant sterns or mr. craig to pinkneyville you said you
wanted me to rite about my close my oald shirts is about wore out one
of them will do to ware a rite smart yet and my white shirt is good
yet   I think I have got close enough to do me til I get to come home
you rote that you sent me a pare of shoes by Brady but he says he did
not bring them it made no adds for I did not need them I have just
had them helf solved I had 3 or fore sides of leather at birleys Tan-
yard one of upper and 3 of saleleathers about 2 I think not taned yet
but there they ort to come out this spring I dont think of any thing
else to rite now I will rite again soon there is a great deal of dissatisfaction about our colonel they dont like him atall I hant got no use
for him he is always drunk when he can get the whiskey he was drunk
the most of the time while we were gone to kentucky nothing more at
present only I remain your affectionate husband til death
John W. Cotton

108 The sheet of paper was torn from a county record book and shows land sales.

Knoxville Tennessee June 22 1863 Dear wife it is again that I take my
pencil in hand to rite you a few lines to try to let you here from me
again I am well and doing well and I hope these lines may find you
the same I hant herd from you since I rote before I am getting very
anxious to here from you all again I no there has letters come for me
but I hant been where I could get them I hant been with the company
since we left James town we were ordered off from there in the nite
and all of the disabled horses and footmen were left behind my horse
wernt able to go with the company on a force march the yankeys got
around us and got ahead of us and got to watburg and burnt our
amunition before we found them out and they went from there to
lanores station on the railroad and burnt up the depot and all of the
cotton and tore up the track it is that they tuck 80 of our regiment
prisoners and parolled them but I dont no who they were it was men
that we left there when we started to kentucky and some of them run
away and went back there the yankeys went from there to knoxville
and our men run them off from there and they went on from there to
wards the strawbery plains above and tore up the railroad and burnt
a little bridge and I hant herd from them since but I think I will here
from them befor I mail this letter our men is after them with a large
force the report is that there is only about twenty five hundred of the
yankeys they are takeing negroes horses and destroying every thing
they can as they go I think if our men lets them get out of here unhurt
they may as well quit I wish they would burn up all of east tennesse
and blot it out of the Southern Confederacy nearly all of the yankeys
that is down here was raised in this state[109] they are looking for reinforcements from above but I dont no whether they have got them or
not they killed a citizen not fare below here they went in to his house
and he resisted them and shot at them and they killed him if I could
see you I could tell you a heap that I cant rite I mite set down and
rite up quire of paper and then I could not tell you all then I cant
think of all I want to rite no how you may still send your letters to
kingston for I dont no where where we will stop I hant herd from asa
but once since I left him at kingston June the 23 I am still well I saw

---

109 It is common knowledge that East Tennessee did not favor secession, and a
mountain state similar to West Virginia would have been formed had it not been
for the prompt action of the Confederate government. One historian says, "Bragg,
in Tennessee, like Washington before Philadelphia, was as much in the land of
enemies as of friends and there were spies and tale-tellers on every side." (A. B.
Moore, *Conscription and Conflict in the Confederacy*, New York: The Macmillan
Co., 1924, p. 148-149) .

mike last nite he was well he is camped not fare from me he is with there waggons there regiment and ourn is gone on after the yankeys I hant herd nothing from them yet it is thought that they have or will get out of the way before we can ham them in I dont no what to rite about it now but I will rite again soon if I get the chance I am in hopes that when the fuss is over and we get settled I will get to come hom I think we will have a chance to come home after horses I had to come back out of Kentucky without a horse it is the worst chance to get a horse in this country that ever I saw nothing more at present only I remain yours til death   John W. Cotton

June the 23 1863 Mariah I will rite a little more I have just received a letter from you were very glad to here from you and to here that you were doing so well I would like to come home and see if you are doing as well as you say you do and get some milk and butter and honey and fryed chicken to eat for we don get that here only as we buy it and it is very hy the most of our men has complained a heap of not getting a plenty to eat since we left kentucky there was three days that we did not draw any rashons but I never suffered I got something every-day I never suffer when there is anything in the country to eat we killed hogs dug irish potatoes and bought meal and I mad out very well and I stopped a sunday and got very good dinner I reckon we will draw a plenty rashons now you spoke of my close You need not bee uneasy about me I will try and get some before I get naked I thought I would not rite you about losing my close in the fite we had but I reckon you will here it any way I lost my saddle bags and my blanket you sent me I hated losing my blanket worse than I did my saddle bags but I hated losing all because they were things you had made for me you need not bee afraid I will get naked I will get close somehow or other I will have a good excuse now to come home I am doing as well as any body you ever saw away from home I do almost as I please I had to come out of kentucky without a horse but my same oald horse toats me yet but he is very pore and weak nothing more I remain your true devoted friend til death   John W. Cotton
I hant herd from dock for some time

Camps near Childresses gap tennessee July the 9 63
Mariah dear wife it is again that I take my pen in hand to rite you a few more line to let you no that I am well and hope these few lines may find you all en joying the same blessing you must excuse me for not riting no sooner I would have rote when nancy left here but I thought

she could tell you more than I could rite and I hant rote since for our officers has been trying to get some of us off home on a detail but they hant got us off yet but I think they will get us off yet for that is all of the chance for our regiment to mount themselves that is what the detail is for if it is made I will bee one of the men that will come home for my horse is no count and horses is very hy here and I reckon not very cheap at home mariah I hant got much to rite to you but if I could see you I could tell you a heap we are camped 11 miles north of knoxville but we will move in a few days on account of forage but we will not move very fare we will bee apt to stay around here some time if the yankeys dont make another rade on tennessee I have received a letter from you since nancy left here it was dated June the 18 you said you had a plenty of rain and your crop looked very well I hope you will bee able to make a good crop you said your were very good but wer bown down I hope they will straten up so they will do to cut I think you can make a good crop you can live another year I got a song ballet from you it is a very good peace of poetry I wouldnt take any thing for it it soots the times the best of any that I have seen I did not no that you had got to bee a poet[110] you said you rote it one nite after weaveing 7 yards of cloth I dont want you to kill your self at work Just because you can you had better work as you can stand it I would rite more if I did not think I would get to come home soon asa I reckon is at home I think we will get our detail yet but Colonel Slaughter says we shouldent come home til we draw our money we may draw in a few days we have sent after our paroles nothing more only I remain you true devoted husband til death   John W Cotton

Alabama Coosa County July the 16   1863
Dear beloved husband it is again I seat my selft to try to rite you a few lines to let you no the children is all well at this time and I hope thes few lins may find you well and doing well I hant much of inportent to rite to you but I thought I wood rite for I expect it will bee som sadfaction to you to here from home if it was only to here we was well I wish I cood here from you every day I wish I node wher you was to day and node you was well but I dont no wher you you are nor what you are a doing you may in a battle now while I am ritin you this letter if I node wher you was in a battle I dont thing I cood set still to rite nor do any thing else but I hope the lorde willbee on your side and gide you saft threw all you trouble and enable you to

110 Unfortunately this "song ballet" is missing.

reach home saft won time mor I hope that happy day will soon com when you can com to see me and you little children I hope the war will con com to a close and you can com home to me to stay it wood bee a day of joy to see you a com home saft again I think if peace was made it wood be the joyfullest times that ever has ben in wood bee to me if you was to com saft I hant here from you sench Nan saw you that has ben too weaks it seem long to me we have a heep of rain corn crapes looks very well but asa can tell you about the [   ] Mrs. holinghead and Jack is gon to see tarrey and mose tha got a letter last sadurday from Mrs mose and she rote that mose was sick and she want come home till he got better I wish you had ben heare to day to have eate dinner with me I hade som beans and a green peach py I have got som ripe peaches tell asa I have made more green peach py tell him I eat all I cood I dont no whether it don him any good not weaver if I only cood see and talk with you won time more I wood bee so glad I cant beegen to tell you any thing about how bad I want to see you I hope that happy day will soon com when I can see you lovely face noth mor I re main you true loving wife till death Mariah Cotton to her dear beloved husband in the war good by my dear husband.[111]

Tennessee Camps near Concord August 7th 1863

Dear beloved wife it is again that I take my pen in hand to let you no that I got back to camps again I got here yesterday I got here with out any trouble I werent bothered any atall on the way it never cost any thing to get here I had meat and bread a plenty to do me to camps when I got here the boys the most of them were gone to jones-borough asa and Porter was both gone they went up on the cars that place is 20 miles above greenville where we went last winter the men that is left here says they dont no what they are gone for I reckon you will here from asa in a few days some of our men went to kentucky and some of them has got back and some hant they got into a battle and got cut all to pieces and some killed and some wounded and some taken prisoners but it is not noun how many they are coming in yet it is thought that 4 or 5 of our company is killed but there cant bee no correct account given about it yet[112] I found our boys very much dishardened and whiped there is a heap of them

[111] In all probability this letter was not mailed because her husband came home on furlough.

[112] Brewer says, "The regiment raided into Kentucky and fought in a half dozen severe conflicts, losing 160 men in all." (Brewer, *Alabama,* 963).

ready to give it up   I am awfully afraid if a change dont take place
soon for the better that we will be whipped[113]   I cant rite much now
for my mind is bothered and the ink I have got to rite with ant no
account at all when I get somethin I can rite with I will rite more[114]
direct your letters to Concord tennessee these lines leave me well my
oald horse has mended up a rite smart since I left him I think I will
by another or swap him in a few days my captain never said anything
about my not bringing no horse back with me there ant but one of our
men got back yet that was sent home with me I was about the first
all the detail that got back nothing more at present I remain your true
devoted husband

John W. Cotton

Camp Big Springs Tennessee August the 13 63
Dear wife I again take my pen in hand to rite you a few more lines to
let you no that I am well and doing well I begin to want to here
from you all again I have not herd from you all since I left home
we have moved from where [we] wer when I first got back from home
we are 12 miles east of Concord there hant no soldiers camped here
before us and our horses have been fareing very well since we come
over here we are camped between two valeys where we can get plenty
of forage for horses if the quarter master does his duty and we can
by any thing in the cuntry to eat cheaper than where we were we are
drawing a plenty to eat now we had a fine mess of beens yesterday
and we have got as fat a turkey to bake for dinner to day as ever you
saw our men has all got back from kentucky but they are killed or
taken prisoners but they are not all killed it is thought that William
Reinolds is killed by a bushwacker and Jim Jacobs is taken prisoner
that is all that you no any thing about if you see Jane Jacobs you may
tell her that her sweet hart is gone up there was a hea (p) of our regiment killed and taken prisoners on there rode into kentucky all that
got back says they dont want to go back there any more I am glad I
wernt here to go with them I lern that mike is gone home they say
dock went home to get a discharge general buckner[115] wont receive no
more substitutes I hope when you read these few lines you may bee

---

113 Following the discouraging military situation numerous "Peace Societies"
were formed in Alabama which influenced both politicians and men in the army
(Fleming, *op. cit.*, 137-138) .

114 With few exceptions the letters are written in ink which is remarkable in
view of the fact that cavalry movements would make it difficult to obtain.

115 Major General Simon B. Buckner.

well and be mor satisfyed than you were when I left you   I hope I
will here from you in a few days this is twice that I have rote since I
got back I hant bought me nary horse yet   I recken we will draw
money today nothing more at present only I remain your true devoted
husband til death   John W. Cotton

Tennessee blunt county August the 18. 1863
My dear beloved wife I take my pen in hand to rite you a few lines to
let you no that I am well and hope these lines may find you all the
same I want to here from you all very bad I hant got nary letter since
I left home I want to here how your hogs is doing and how things is
a doing in general I would bee glad to see you al again a redy I hant
got but little to rite to you I will send this in a letter with asa all of
our foot men is sent to knoxville only those who had the money to
by them a horse to bee mounted on government horses but some
thinks they will bee put into infantry porter went with them and went
off sick he had been sick two or three days but was better me nor asa
hant got no horses yet I bargained for one but failed to get him I aim
to go out into the cuntry in a short time and swap my ould horse off
for a good one we have drawed money since I got back and I got all
the boys was oweing me but twenty dollars and I hant seen the man
that ows that since we drawed our money I have got about a hundred
and fifteen dollars since I got back to my company if your hogs ant all
dead   you had better have them fed about once a day with green
corn give them about one stalk a piece a day I think that meat will bee
of more value than corn and you should make your hogs do as well as
you can I have nearly got in the notion if I can get in a substitute to
get one and come home and still this winter doctor moon is here now
trying to get in a substitute if he gets him in I will let you no and I
will rite all about it I will rite again soon if ould man kelly ant gone
to the war tell him if he is working at the still if I can fix my business rite I will want him to substitute for me six months[116] nothing
more at present only I remain your til death John W Cotton

Tennessee Camps Bells bridge August 25th 1863
Dear beloved wife I take my pen in hand to rite you a few lines to let
you no that I have just received a letter from you for the first time

---

[116] Substitutes from beyond the age limit (35) were allowed "under such regula-
tions as may be prescribed by the Secretary of War" (Statutes, II, 29-32, April 16,
1862).   This law was changed in 1863 to prevent any substitution (Journal of the
Congress of the Confederate States, III, 499, on December 28, 1863).

since I left home it was mailed August the 19 I was very sorry to here
that ann was sick but was glad to here that the rest of you were well
you never said what was the matter with ann I hope you will rite in
your next letter what was ailding her I hope she is better by this time
these lines leave me well and herty   nearly all the boys is sick that
went home when I did but I have been as harty as I ever was in my
life   I hope when you reed these lines you will all bee enjoying the
same blessing that I have we have moved again from big springs to
bells bridge 9 miles west of knoxville we are expecting a fite some
where not fare from here they say the yankeys are aiming to try to
take east tennessee and everything is a perfect stir they are sending
reinforcements from virginey to our assistance there is but a few of
our regiments from here   only those that have disable horses and
them that are a foot all of our briggade that had serviceable horses
are about 10 miles from here on clinch river awaiting for the yankeys
to come on and attact them   I have herd that they were in 8 miles of
kingston they have moved all of the sick out of knoxville that were
able to bee moved and lots of the citizens are moving out of the town
everything is in a perfect stir but I think if the yankeys comes in here
we will whip them badly   I have just swoped off my ould horse for a
very pretty little mule and give $200 to boot   I would like to have it
at home   it was 3 years oald last spring   I would be glad to here from
you again soon there has been for of company deserted since I came
back from home nothing more only I remain your til death   John W.
Cotton

Tennessee Camp near Loudon Aug 30th (1863)
Dear beloved wife and children
once more take my pen in hand to try to let you no that I am well
and I hope these few lines may reach you the same I have not herd
from you since I wrote before I have not got but one letter from you
since I left home but every thing has been in such a stir that we have
not got the mail regular we have moved three times since I rote my
other letter we have been traveling nearly all of the time we are now
in camp 4 miles below loudon we moved here this morning I dont
know how long we will stay here our horses were inspected yesterday
and a heap of our horses were condemned and turned over to the quarter master to sell and a heap of them pronounced not able for service
and sent off to a paster to mend up my mule was sent with them its
sholders were hurt with the saddle and it was lame footed they were
all put in an old dry paster and a gard put own them they will perish

if they dont feed them there is a talk of all that is dismounted being put in the infantry the men all swares that if they do put them in the infantry they will go home   some left last nite colonel good says that his men shant bee treated in no such way he says he wont stay in the brigade no longer he was sent to Jacks borough to relieve a regiment and when he got there the regiment was gone and the town was full of yankeys and our men rode rite up to them in speaking distance before they found them out and they made a charge on our men and they broke to run and the yankeys after them and they run them about 10 miles and killed some of them and tuck some prisoners but we never lost maney out of our company I went with them he only had 75 or 80 men with him alfred deason run his horse til he died in the road they run their horses 15 miles they had like to have killed all of there horses some lost there hats guns blankets close and some there horses I herd that the yankeys is almost 15 miles of huntsville our men have give up huntsville and moved all of the government propperty out of it[117] they are planning for a big fite here at loudon there is a heap of troops here and they are still comeing on every train some think the big fite will be some where about Chattanooga I think if they will come here they will ketch a general flogging the most of us have gest been to the paster and got our horses since I commenced riting I aim to swop my mule off for a horse as soon as I get the chance I saw frank worthen the other day and he said he was discharged and gone home he said John tramel was not very will they are going to move clost to us dock hant come to us yet I hant herd from him since he was with the company I rote to him but hant got no answer yet I want to here from home very bad and I am afraid that I will have to here that ann is no better but wourse but I have to live in hopes that she is better and all of the rest well I wish I had some of your peech brandy to drink I think if would help me rite how much you make   I cant tell you what to do about hireing oald man kelly yet doctor moon has been here more than two weaks and he hant got his substitute in yet if our regiment gets out of the briggade I will try to put in a substitute the papers wont have to go no further then than colonel good now they have to go to general buckner   nothing more   J W Cotton

117 Huntsville, Alabama, was not completely evacuated until August 31, the next day, but rumors had been going for days that the "Feds" were leaving. For a very lively contemporary account of the period see Mrs. W. D. Chadick, "*Civil War Days in Huntsville, The Complete Diary of Mrs. W. D. Chadick,*" *The Huntsville Times,* (N.d.) . This diary begins April 11, 1862 when General Mitchell took possession of city and continues to May 26, 1865.

Tennessee Camps near Charleston September the 4 1863
It is again dear wife that I seat myself to try to rite you a few lines to
let you no that I am well and hope these lines may find you well I
am very uneasy about home I have not got but the one letter from you
since I left home I am very anxious to here from ann but it is very
uncertain when I will get another letter everything is so tangles up
the post master here at charleston says there hant been no mail in two
or three days our troops have all fell back to this place they have burnt
loudon bridge and distroyed all of the flats and canoes to prevent the
yankeys from crossing tennessee river we here they are still follwing
after no they were said to bee in 15 miles of this place and was trying
to cut off our rear our briggade covered the retreat and they were
trying to cut them off I dont think we will make much of a stand here
nor I dont no where we will make a permanent stand but I think there
will bee one of the hardest battles fought here that has ever been
fought they say we have got over one hundred thousand men round[118]
about here I have not been with the regiment for several days til this
morning I have been detailed to drive some ould horses and there is
only a few of us here there is some of us here and some back with the
briggade and some that is dismounted at town two miles from here I
dont think there is any danger of my beeing in to a fite yet a while
for our regiment is so badly scattered that I dont think it will bee
put in to a fite til it gets to gether I dont want you to bee uneasy
about me but take good care of yourself and the children I would give
a heap if I could get a letter rite straight from home I dont no where
to tell you to di rect your letters to but you may rite to Charleston
tennesse if we fall back they will bee sent back to us I may get a
letter if I ever get to see the captain I shall bee uneasy about ann til
I here she is well nothing more at present I re main your tru devoted
husband til death John W Cotton I will rite again soon as I can.

Calhone Georgia September 11th 63
Dear beloved wife and children I will try to rite you a few lines to
let you no that I am well but very uneasy eye have not herd from
home yet I am very uneasy about ann and I cant here from her I

118 The Chickamauga Campaign lasted from August 16 to September 22. The reports of the Confederate operations may be found in *Official Records,* Series I, III,
Part II. Estimates of number vary greatly. Horn quotes General Joe Wheeler
giving "Rosecrams, 72, 603 and Bragg 46,000 actually engaged" and Livemore's figure giving Union strength as 58,222 and Confederate 66,326, Horn himself does not
believe Bragg had more than 50,000 (*Army of Tennessee,* 273). The 10th Confederate Cavalry fought under Forrest "and lost heavily" (Brewer, *Alabama,* 693).

wood be glad to here that she was well we have not got much mail in about a weak and I dont no when we will get any I reckon not til the fite is over I expect it will bee at rome georgia I am now at Calhone on my way to rome rome is about 120 miles from home our hole armey has left tennessee but I herd this morning that longstreet[119] had retaken knoxville and 8,000 yankeys they are agoing to have a big fite soon and I think we will whip them there is a heap soldiers deserting more tennesseans than any body else there is 15 of our company deserted I cant rite but little now for I hant got time I have only stopped to rest I hope these few lines find you well and doing well I shall bee uneasy about Ann until I here that she is well direct your next letter to rome georgia I would love to see you all again already but dont bee uneasy about me I think if we get whiped in this fite the war will soon end[120] nothing more at the present take good care of yourself til I come to see you again I will rite again soon

John W. Cotton

Tennessee Camps 15 miles north west of dalton 7 miles south of ringgold september the 16. 1863 once more dear wife I take my pen in hand to rite you a few lines to let you no that I have not herd from you all yet and I am very uneasy about home and about ann she may bee well or she may bee dead I cant here we dont get any mail at all nor I dont no when we will you dont no how bad I want to here from home we have been to rome since I rote to you we only stayed there one nite and were ordered back to dalton we stayed there all nite then come here we are 15 miles north west of dalton we stayed camped on the battle field where they had a fite last saturday[121] we lost 5 men and the yankeys 17 killed we taken some fifty prisoners we had only one regiment in the fite and I dont no how many yankeys we we whiped them they are about three miles from here now we expect to fite every day the first georgia had a skirmich with them today they tryed to take some yankey wagons but failed I expect we will bee into it before many days there will bee a big fite before many days some where between here and rome and I expect it will be the worst battle that has ever been fought in this war they say we have got the largest armey there has ever been together since this was commenced and I feel confident

---

119 General James Longstreet.

120 Although Cotton had not always been optimistic this is the first admission of possible defeat. On September 16, however, he was sure the Confederates would win.

121 This battle is not recorded in the official records.

that we will whip the fite if we do I think that it will bring about
peace there has been several small fites with the cavalry and we have
drove them back it was thought 3 days ago that they were retreeting
back across tennessee river but they dont think so now we keep heering
that longstreet have retaken knoxville and a number of prisoners if
that is so it will help us out a heap I saw albert martin today he was
well he says he wants me to get a transfer to his regiment I hant seen
John Tramel yet I saw homes waldrop day before yesterday he was
well albert martin says his wife has three children and dock[122] cant
walk yet without his crutches but can ride anywhere he wants to he is
overseeing for frank worthen and is getting along very well he told me
that John Hindsman were dead he was killed at vixburg I had not
herd of it before nor I dont no whether you have or not I rote to you
that mike was discharged and gone home I hant herd from dock yet we
have got only ten men here with us to go into a fite we have got fifteen
gone home I am riting this letter but I dont no when I will get to send
it I will try to send it off tomorrow asa blade says he is going to dalton
tomorrow if he can get off I wish I had some of your good brandy to
drink I think it would help my feelings and maby I wouldnt study so
much about home but if I could only here from home it would help
me more than brandy I would like to no how things is going on in
general how your hogs is doing and how manuel is getting on pulling
fodder and how much brandy you maid and whether par had to pay
tax for stilling not who paid it and how much he charged you for
stilling your peaches these lines leave me well but very uneasy I hope
when they come to hand they may find you all well and enjoying
your selves very well mariah dont bee uneasy about me but if I should
get into a battle and get killed do the best you can for yourself and
the children but I hope to live to see this war ended and return home
to you and your dear little ones and that we may live a long and
hapy life and that I may live to bee a beter man nothing more at
present   John W Cotton

send your letters to dalton georgia and maby they will follow us
Camps near Chattanooga September the 24. 63
Dear beloved wife and children I again take my pen in hand try to
rite you a few lines to let you no that I am well and still alive and live
in hopes that these lines may reach you the same I hant got but little

---

122 It is difficult to keep up with "Dock's" location, but here he seems to be in
Georgia.

time to rite our adjutant is going to dalton and I will try to send this
by him I reckon you will here of the big battle[123] we have had before
you get this letter I hant got time to rite much about it now but we
have given them the worst whipping they ever had so ther prisoner
say we have run them all out of georgia and they have run them all
across the tennessee but one corpse they say they will have to cross but
they say they are in there fort at chattanooga and will give us another
fite be fore they cross our cavalry cant do not more good here so we
will go back to east tennessee I think in a few days if we dont start
today I here that our men has whipped them there they will all have
to go back to kentucky the fite has been going on 6 days and is still
going on our regiment has been into it and around where they were
fiting all the time we brought on the fite saturday morning but our
regiment hant lost but few men our company hant lost nary man killed
or wounded but I cant see how we all escapted we were suppoting a
battery on sunday evening and the yankeys commenced a cross fire on
it and the grape shot shells fell around us like hail but we got behind
trees and places so none of us did not get hurt they shot off three
horses lags clost to us and killed one man and wounded one if I could
tell you all I have seen it would make your heart ache to think of it
but I could not tell if half as bad as it is nothing more at present
John W Cotton

Tennessee Camps near Chattanooga September the 29. 1863
Dear and most beloved wife and family I once more take my pen in
hand to try to rite you a few more lines to try to let you no where I
am and what I am doing I am well and doing as well as any can in the
place I am in our regiment is in site of the yankeys all the time and
have been for fore days they are in there brest works here at chattanooga[124] and we are standing picket around them in gun shot of them
and we have some fireing backwards and forwards at them but they
wont come out nor we wont go to them our men are planting there
cannons as fast as they can to try to shell them out of there brest
works but I dont no how they will come out we have got the advan-
tage of a big hill to shell them from and the lookout mountain we can
here there drums and fifes and horns and here them crossing the river

[123] The battle at Chickamauga, Georgia, was fought on September 19-20 (*Official
Records* series 1, XXX, part I).
[124] General Bragg was severely censured for his handling of the Chickamauga,
Chattanooga Campaigns. See Horn, *Army of Tennessee*, chapter VV and *Official
Records*, Series, XXX, Part II.

on there pontoon bridge and we can go out on a big hill and see all
over there fortifications and them too they say that there is a heap of
our forces crossing the river to cut them off from there pervisions but
I dont no how many I think ould brag is trying to get them out of
chattanooga without a fite if he can it will bee the best for if we have
to whip them out we will loose a many a man and mayby get whiped
I think they are fortifying on the other side of the river it may bee
some time before we get them away from here if we get them away at
all I wish you could bee here to see them and there fortifications
there hant been no fiting here only picket fiting in about five days
and they say our men has got 150 canons planted to shell the yankeys
out of town and I herd that they wer a going to commence shelling
them today at 9 oclock but they hant commenced it yet I reckon we
will leave here and let the infantry take our place there is a heap more
cavalry here besides our regiment I stood picket the other nite in
shooting distance of the yankeys there was three of us on the same post
and one stood while the others slept the yankeys say we have whiped
them the worst they ever have been I reckon I have said enough about
the yankeys I had rather reed a letter from you than rite about them
a weak I have not got nary letter from you yet and there ant no use in
trying to tell how bad I want to here from you all I want to here
whether you have got manuel for another year or not and how you are
all getting on in general and if you can hire ould man kelly or not to
take my place if you could I would try to find out whether he would
bee received or not before he come but there will be no chance to get
him in til this fierse is over if at all I wish I had some of your brandy
here I could sell it at any price I would ask for it I have swaped my
little mule a way and got a fine young iron gray horse 4 years ould
and give $175 to boot you ort to see him I think if we both live til the
war ends I will bring him home but I am afraid it will be a long time
yet I saw John tramel the other day and he said mike was comeing
back to his company phelix got him a substitute and went to the infantry and they told him they would receive his substitute and they
mustered him in and his substitute was not received and he is in the
infantry yet and was taken prisoner at cumberland gap I dont no what
to rite unless I could here from you direct your next letter to tennessee
Chickamogga station nothing more at present only I remain your true
devoted husband til death dont bee uneasy about me
                                 John W Cotton

Tennessee Chicamauga Creek Oct 5th 1863
dear beloved wife I have received a letter from you at last I was ex-
tremely glad to here from you all but it gave me much dessatisfaction
to here that you had been sick but was glad to here that you was better
and I was glad to here that ann had got well you never said what ailded
you nor ann I would like to no what ailded you both I am afraid
you wont take as much care of yourself as you ort to I dont want
you to expose yourself no more than you can help keep out of the dew
and rain and coalds we have some very coal weather here for the sea-
son we had a killing frost the 20 and 21 of october [sic] and we are
having some frost now you never said anything about hireing manuel I would bee glad of your hireing him I want you to hire him let
the price bee what it may I was sorry to here of your loosing so many
of your hogs but was glad it wernt no worse I think you got a good
price for your cow you said you wanted to no whether you must kill
that steer or sell him if you need the beef kill him if you dont sell him
rite to me whether the concript will take par or not they say here that
it takes all up to fifty and down to 17 for confederate service and
from 50 to 60 for state service[125] and I want you to tell me how much
tax you have to pay you said you could not sell the brandy without
paying tax on it if you do not need money keep it and maybe I will
get the chance to sell it myself there is talk of colonel slaughter
drawing his batallion from the regiment and moving it to talladega
but that is too good nuse to bee sow but him and good is very much at
outs I reckon you have not forgot where I told you to have wheat
soad have it soad the last of this month if you can the letter I get was
dated the 26 of september these few liens leave me well but uneasy
about you I would bee better satisfied if I new what ailded you[126] I
hope these lines may reach you soon and find you improving and all
of the rest well I am glad you have weaned little ginea I would love
to be at home the best you ever saw but there is no chance to come
home now rite often and let me no how you are getting on we are expecting a fite here every day oald brag is still planting his canon[127] to
shell the yankeys out of chattanooga we wont have anything to do
with it til they get them out of town nothing more at present
                                                        John W Cotton

125 The second conscription act changed the ages from 18 to 35 to 17 to 45 and
not 50, as Cotton says here. As he says here those above 45 were liable to state service. His father, Cary Cotton, was born in 1802 so he is now 61.
126 As is revealed (October 28) Mrs. Cotton was pregnant.
127 He probably refers to Lookout Mountain.

Tennessee Chicanorga Camps October 11th 1863

Most dear beloved wife I this eavning take the pleasure of riting you a few lines to try to let you no that I am well and hope these lines may reach you in due time and find you all well and doing well Mariah I hope you are still on the mend and if not well soon will bee I hope you will not expose yourself so as not to make against you I want to here from you very bad I have got but the one letter from you yet but am looking for another everyday I am very uneasy about you and will bee until I here that you are well I no from the way you rote before that you were not out of danger I was very well satisfied about home until I herd that you and ann was sick I am afraid the next time I here from home some of the rest of you will be sick you said you wanted me to rite whether I wanted you to make me any close or not I dont want you to make me any I have got a plenty and when they wear out I will draw more I can draw them cheaper than you can make them and I think you have got as many at home as you can make for any how I hant got no nuse to rite to you only I herd the report of canon on the other side of the river this morning I suppose some of our men has gone around and got in the rear of the yankeys and they were fiting but the fireing has seased or gone out of hearing everything is still at chattanooga we are about three miles from chattanooga picketing on the river to keep the yankeys from crossing and they are picketing the other side to keep us from crossing Mike nor dock hant come back yet some of our men that run away and went home has got back and we here that some of them are on the way I think the most of them will come back   I would like to no whether you have got manuel for another year or not and whether you hogs that is alive lookes like they will ever be any account or not but above all I would rather here how you are getting nothing more at present I remain your true devoted husband til death   John W Cotton

them notes of oald Stephen Thomases I want you to give to par or some body else to collect them if he hant paid them   Can oald sweat or little giney talk yet

Tennessee Camp near Chattanooga Oct the 19th 1863

Mariah Dear beloved wife and children I again take my pen in hand to try to rite you a few lines to let you no that I am well all but a little touch of the diarhea I hope these few lines may reach you in diew time and find you all well it is strange to me that I cant get a letter from you I have only got one from you yet it was mailed the 26 of September we send off mail every day but dont get any hardly I dont no what becomes of them for I no you rite to me I would give any thing to here from you again I want to no how you are getting along I am afraid you hant got well yet and I am afraid that some of the other children has been sick since I herd from home Asa has got back to the company again he says he dont get no letter neither he is well I dont no what to rite unless I could here from home I have got a stray mule that I tuck up on picket two weaks (I will send you a pen) agao if the owner dont come and get it I will let Asa have it he is riding it now it is worth fore hundred dollars I think it is a government mule but it is not branded I dont think there is any danger of the owner comeing after it there was two horses with it and they come and got them and never said any thing about the mule times are stil here yet there is no fiting going on yet 10 of our men swam across the tennessee river and caught two yankey cariers and a dispach and it said so I her that if they did not get reinforcements in 10 days they would have to fall back from chattanooga we moved back nite before last to there brestworks to stand picket round them we stand in two or three hundred yard of them in an ope oald field direct your next letter to chattanooga and maby I will get them oald good is gone home on a furlow I here that he is going to see the govner of georgia and try to git to go down in georgia to gard some salt works nothing more   John W. Cotton

Tennessee Camps near Chattanooga October the 25. 63
Dearest and most dily beloved wife again I take my pen in hand to try to rite you a few lines to try to let you no that I am well and hop these few lines may come to hand and find you all well and doing well I was glad to reed a letter from nan to asa she said she was at your house and you were all well except bad colds you had better believe that I was glad to here that you had got well she said Mike and Sally[128] was at your house that was something that I did not expect to here of I recken it done you a rite smart of good to see them come I like to have been at home when they comed I have not got nary letter from you yet but I keep looking for one every day for we have an every day mail I would like to bee at home now to help saw wheat and gather corn and see to things in general I would bee glad to no whether you have hired manuel yet or not I had rather you would buy him for I think you could raise money enough to pay for him tell me how much corn you make and how much you have to give to the govern-

[128] This must be Mrs. Cotton's brother and sister.

ment[129] and rite all of the nuse and rite how sack[130] like alabama and
how she thinks you are getting along and tell me all you can think of
and so on we have had a site of rain for the last fore or five weaks
our camps are very mudy but apart of our regiment has left here this
morning for harison 10 miles from here our squadron is left here to
stand picket three days the then we are going and one of the other
squadron will come here to take our place we are still clost to them but
they are very peaceable they threw a few shells at our infantry a few
days ago ould general brag has issued an order and says that he will
give any man a 40 day furlow if he will a a recruit to his company
I want you to see fil coker and see if he intends to come to our company and if he does tell him I want him to come as a recruit for so I
can get a furlow and I will do all I can for him in any way possible
and bee more than fifteen hundred times abliged to him if he does
come to go to goodgame and have his name inrolled and get a showing from him so that he wont bee bothered on his way up here tell
him he well never find a better regiment nor one that has more privilege   nothing more at present only I remain your affectionate husband til death John W. Cotton to his wife and children I love to bee at
home a while and I would like better to bee at home all the time ould
Jef davis has been up here and made a speech and said peace would
bee made in six months[131]

Tennessee Camps near Chicamatiga October 28 1863
Dear beloved wife and children   I take my pen in hand this morning
to try to ancer your kind letter which I received last nite it was dated
the 20 it gave me much pleasure to here from you and to here the
children were all well and it gives me much displeasure to here of
your sickness and to here what caused it   I was a little astonished to
here of your undertaking to throw up fodder and you in the condition
you were in   it looks like you mite have nown it would have hurt you
but you will always do too much but I hope you will do less hereafter

129 On July 1, 1863, a tax of 8 per cent on all agricultural products was passed
(quoted in Fleming, op. cit., 172).
130 "Sack" and "Sally" are used enterchangably.   Both Mr. and Mrs. Cotton had
a sister Nancy and a sister Sarah, probably on both sides named for the same people.
Their grandmother Cotton was named Sarah and her husband was Weaver Cotton
(Deed Book E. [Coweta County] p. 72, settlement of the estate of Weaver Cotton).
131 One of the stock criticisms against Jefferson Davis as president of the Confederacy is that he constantly interfered with military operations by giving direct orders and by visiting felids of operations.   This charge is denied by Rembert W. Pat-
rick in *Jefferson Davis and His Cabinet* (L.S.U. Press 1944) but he does say that
Davis "save for a few instances never visited a battlefield except upon the invitation
of the commanding officer." p. 32.

and take better care of yourself these lines leave me well and I hope they may reach you in dieu time and find you all well and doing well you said you had not hired manuel yet but you herd he was to hire if he is I think you can hire him you said you had paid part of your tax I think they are very hy and it looks hart too to think a soldier that has to hire a crop made has to give a tenth of it to the government and him in the field fiting to sustain it but if the tax would sustain it I would be willing to pay as much more you rote to me about oald man kelley substituting for me I talked to the captain this morning and he says he thinks it will bee a bad chance for me to put him in as all the big officers is down upon substituting but colonel good is at home now but he will be back in a few days and I will see him or get the captain to see him about it and I will rite all about it I did not understand from your letter whether he was willing to come for during the war at the rates of seven hundred dollars for six months or for just a few months we have moved out from chattanooga so we will be more handy to forage but we send one squadron in at a time to stand gard and it stays three days at a time the pickets got to fiting and the yankeys come out of the brestworks and our men it is said whiped them back but I ant herd with what result our squadron has just left while they were fiting the fite was on the fur side of the brestworks from us none of our regiment went in it nothing more at present only I remain your true devoted husband til death   J. W. Cotton

rite in your next letter if vardiman and them is making whiskey and if any body else is making any and what the tax is one making whiskey and if the law allows them to make it now I dont want you to make me any close til I rite for them if I need them I will draw them Can Sweet and Jiney talk yet

October 29 1863
Mariah I will rite a few more lines this morning before I send my letter off I am as well as common   they are still canonadnig at chattanooga they were at it all day yeasterday and they commenced last nite after midnite and they are at it yet it is about sunup I here that day before yesterday the yankeys tuck the 15 alabama regiment and we tuck seven hundred prisoners from them I hant herd whether they fought yesterday with small arms or not I think they will decide the fite now before they quit we will have to go back tomorrow or next day on picket nothing more at this time I hope you are well
John W. Cotton

Camp near Chicamorga Tennessee November 3th 1863
Most dear beloved wife I have just received a letter from you a few
minutes ago I was very glad to here from you all but I was very sorry
to here that you had not got well yet   You said you had just put in a
peace of cloth   I am afraid you will go to weaving before you are
able   I think I know what ailed you by the way you rote I am sorry
that you had such bad luck and I am sorry to think that my coming
home a few days caused you to suffer so much   I had rather not come
home atall but I dont no when I will ever get to come home again[132]
I hope when you get these lines you may be well   they leave me well
and we are still here clost to the yankeys our camps ant more than a
mild apart but the river is between us   they are still shelling away at
chattanooga they have been fiting there 9 days but they hant fought
any one the side where we stand picket it is five or six miles from here
to chattanooga but we go there to stand picket we stand two days and
are off fore but when we ant at chattanooga we stand picket at the
river so we are busy all the time   we have a heap of rain but the
weather is pleasant we hant had much frost yet   you said you could
get oald man kelley to take my place for six months for seven hundred
dollars if I can put him in my place I will do it but I cant tell til
oald colonel good comes back I will see him as soon as he comes back
and see whether any body is allowed to still or not and if vardaman
and webb and carlisle is stilling if they are and I get to come to still
this winter if I could I could make more money than I ever have in
all my life I hope you will hire manuel nothing more at present I
remain your husband til death   John W Cotton

Tennessee Camps near Chicamooga Nov the 10 1863
Dear beloved wife I again take my pen in hand to try to rite you a
few lines in ancer to you kind letters I have just received yesterday
one was dated August the 31 and one October the 28 and 29 I red
them with much pleasure I was glad to here from you again but I was
very sorry to think you were not well but I hope by the time you get
this letter you will bee well again I was glad to here that the children
was well and I was glad to here you were done gathering corn I think
you have made a very good crop of corn and I hope you will get your
wheat sowed in good time I hate for you to pay the 10 of your corn

132 This statement led to the only misunderstanding between Mr. and Mrs. Cotton
in these letters. The letter to Mrs. Cotton on December 9 shows how this statement
was interpreted more literally than the writer intended.

to the government[133] I want you from this out to sell everything you
have to sell for all you can and I want you to hire manuel for next
year let him cost what he may for if you were to miss a crop it would
ruin you for you would not bee able to by your pervisions corn is
worth 7 or 8 per bushel here now if you have any to sell dont sell it
yet you ort to feed your hogs well and make them very fat and keep
you stock hogs fat and I wont you to tell manual I want him to tend
to mary and get her fat this winter and not let nobody steel her I
here they are steeling horses down there hold on to your brandy till
all the rest is sold in the cuntry and you can get anything you will
ask for it I have got my mule yet that I tuck up on picket we have
been relieved from standing picket at chattanooga we are now standing picket on the river not fare from our camps there is more soldiers
comeing here from virgini and some going from here to up about
louden and knoxville I think that there will bee another fite here
before long or else ould brag will try to flank them there is a heap of
them at chattanooga I left there sunday morning and this is tuesday
and the boys talks to them across the river here everyday they want
tobacco very bad but our boys wont let them have it our men swaps
papers with them ever once and a while[134] they seam to bee very
friendly with us it is thought that they are very scarce of pervisions I
dont think they can stay here long if they dont get possession of the
lookout mountain and the river below chattanooga it has been raining a heap and the roads must bee very bad and they have to have
everything they get but it has fared off and turned cold it was very
cold last nite there was a heap of ice this morning you said mike and
sally has been too see you I think it is a wonder that sack tuck a notion to come to see you you said mike was comeing back to his company as soon as he gets able they are gone up in east tennessee they say
we are not in there briggade now they say we are under a man by the
name of martin[135] one company of our regiment is gone to escort a
general Marion bates and bill bates belongs to that company they are

133 A tax in kind of ten per cent was placed on wheat, corn, oats, rye, potatoes
but a man could reserve 100 bushels of corn and 30 bushels of the others for his own
use. This seems to be the law at the time this letter was written but it was amend-
ed many times (Coulter, *Confederate States*, 178-179).
134 In view of the fact there was no censorship, North or South, it is little short
of a miracle that an army or any part of it was ever surprised. At least one Confederate general went so far as to subscribe to Union papers that were relayed to
him through Kentucky. In this way he knew many moves of the enemy.
135 General W. H. Martin of Arkansas.

both well they have herd that uncle matt is dead I herd some time ago that John hindsman was dead but never herd that nuce wilson had his arm shot off nor of the rest that are wounded you said the cavalry had bring two men but never said who they were I cont think there is much deserting a going on now I think the most that is deserting from here is tennesseeans some of our regiment gos home but they dont stay long before they come back you said Caroline had not herd from bill in two months asa went to his regiment about two weeks ago and saw him he was well and fat but I reckon he rote about seeing him before now his regiment was in the line of battle in site of chattanooga I would er went to see him but I did not get the chance you said you got 26 gallons of brandy I would like to no why you did not get any mor there is something rong about it   these lines leave me well and hopeing they may reach you in diew time and find you well but I am afraid from what you say that you wont bee well till your 9 months is out I dont want you to do anything to hurt yourself any more you said that sweat couldnt talk any better yet I wish I could here little giney talk and say par tell sweet if he don talk I wont give him no candy when I come home I will give it all to giney but if he will talk I will give him some two you rote a heap about my putting ould man kelly in as a substitute I cant tell you anything about it yet colonel good has come back but I hant had the chance to see him about it yet I am on picket every other day I am on picket now setting on the bank of the river riting nothing more at present John W Cotton I will see ould good soon or get the Capt to see him for me and I will rite all about but it is a bad chance

Tennessee Camps near blew springs Nov 18th 1863
Dear beloved wife and children I again take my pen in hand to rite you a few more lines in answer to your kind letters which I have received since I rote to you one was rote when mike was at your house and one november the 3 and the other I dont recollect the date I have got several ould letters here lately I have been getting letters tolerable regular now for a while I hope I will keep getting them I hate to here that your are unwell in every letter I reed and I am glad to here that the children is well I am glad to here that your hogs is doing well now how many have you got to kill is nother of your sows dyed since I left home how many shoats have you got left how did your pees turn out you ort to make your killing hogs very fat for pork and bacon will bee very hy how is mary comeing on we have moved from where we were camped up the river about 10 miles near a place called blew springs

but we are still picketing on the tennessee river but our duty ant as heavy as it were before but since we have moved here we have to drill twice a day and then go on dress perraid in the eavning and we have very strict orders I have got my mule yet my horse looks very well he has mended a rite smart since I got him but I am afraid that corn will soon get so scarce I cant get any only what I draw but we are getting plenty now and there is a plenty of hogs about here we are put in another briggade[136] there has been another detail made to go home to by horses Asa is on the detail I dont no when they will get off November the 19 these lines leave me well and hopeing they may reach you in due time and find you well and doing well we have got to move again today 3 miles further up the river you will still send your letters to the same place till you here from me I will let you no when to change them nothing more at present I remain your true devoted husband til death John W. Cotton

Jasper Tennessee Novemer the 26. 1863 Dear Wife I once more take my pen in hand to rite you a few lines to let you no where I am and to let you no that I am well and doing well we have plenty to eat and tolerable plenty for our horses we find corn very scarce in places we have to press the most of our corn it is selling from $1.50 cts to $2.00 perbushel we pressed some yesterday that had tell sold at $2.00 per bushel as to fodder we hardly ever get any Asa is well but william is not he is rite sick he has bee complaining several days I think he will come home before long if he dont get a heap better his sold complaint is working on him and he has got the dirhoea very bad Asa looks as well as you ever saw him and I am as fat as you ever saw me I hope these few lines may find you all enjoying the same good blessing Mariah I would bee happy to to no that you and the children were all enjoying as good health as I am at present I would bee glad to here from you all now I hant much to rite to you we had a very ruff trip from chattanooa over here it is a very rough road and we had to cross the tennesse river in the nite we were from about 8 oclock in the nite til about sun up nect morning our company crossed first and we went about a mild and camped til the rest got over we got here last nite we were two days comeing we may stay here a few days lent I dont no how long I will not rite no more now I will finish in the morning it is time to commence about supper now and I may get some more news by morning how long we will stay have (turnover) November the 27

136 This is probably Wade's brigade (Brewer, *Alabama*, 693).

Mariah my dear I cant find out any thing about when we will leave
here William is no better yet I am still well Asa says tell you that he is
well setting up washing the dishes the company is generally well I
would bee glad to see you all very and see how you all were getting
along but I dont no when I will get to come to see you all you must not
grieve nor trouble you self about me for I am doing better than you are
I am doing as well as I could wish to do in the war I want you to enjoy
yourself as though I were at home to go see you neighbours and get
them to come to see you and I will come to see you as soon as I can
get a furlow there is several of our battalion deserted from camps and
one of our company you need not look for me til you see me comeing
I am going to start to bridge port now in a few minutes to see if I can
get a letter from you it is 12 miles we herd before we got here that it
was only 5 miles but I dont mind riding five miles to here from you
all nothing more at present only remain you affectionate husband til
death fare well til I rite to you again

John W Cotton
to Mariah Cotton

Georgia Camps near dalton November the 29. 1863
Dear beloved wife I again take my pen in hand to rite you a few lines
to try to rite you a few lines to try to let you no that I am well and
hope these few lines may find you all enjoying the same blessing I
hant rote to you in more than a weak we have been riding almost day
and nite for 8 days we have been riding up and down tennessee river
the most of the time trying to keep the yankeys from crossing but
they crossed anyhow we went to east tennessee and they crossed at the
mouth of chicamauga and we was ordered back and we found them at
cleavlen day before yesterday morning and we had a fite with them
that lasted about two hours and we whiped them and made them
skedaddle in a hurry they left horses mules saddles bridles and pervisions cooking things and they strowed everything as they went I shall
have to quit riting for I am detailed to go off on duty but I dont no
what I never got hurt nor none of our company colonel slaughter
was wounded in the shoulder[137] I dont think I will be able to put
ould man kelly in any place give twelve hundred dollars for manuel if
you can by him for me less if I can sell my mule and draw money I
can send you five or six hundred dollars I would rite more but I hant

---

137 While Cotton does not say anything about it, Col. Goode was wounded about
the same time at Chickamauga (Brewer, *Alabama*, 693) .

got the time now Braggs armey is falling back from chatta nooga again they are at dalton the most of them I dont no where he will make another stand nothing more I will rite again soon John W Cotton

Georgia Camps near dalton December the 9. 1863?
Dear beloved wife I again take my pen in hand to rite you a few lines to try to ancer your kind letter I have received from you since I rote to you I rote to you the 30 of last month but did not have time to rite but little I thought then I would have time to rite again soon but I was sent off on detail to gard some forage and was gone 4 days and then as soon as I got back the regiment was ordered off and so this is the first time I have had the chance to rite I am expecting to here the word saddle every minute I hant got much to rite to you but if I could see you I could tell you a heap you said in one of your letters that I said in one of mine that I did not want to come home any more I think you must have been mistaken in reeding my letter if I rote that to you I did not aim to do it[138] god nose if I dont want to come home nobody never did I dont want you to think that I dont want to come home you said you wanted me to come home by christmas I would like to come the worst you ever saw but I dont see any chance to get home but I recken Asa will bee at home soon on his detail if he comes home you may send me a pare of pants by him you said cohen and Medill and david martin was comeing to our company if any one of them comes as a recruit for me I will try to get a furlow I am a fraid you wont hire manuel I want you to hire him let him cost what he may you said you wanted to hare if eye could get kelly in my place we have so much running about to do that I hant had the chance to find out I have almost give out trying to get him in if you cant by manuel I want you to get par to by you a negro girl if he can find one to by if you hant got money enough I can get a plenty by selling my mule and by your selling you brandy nothing more at present I remain yours truly J W Cotton

16 I am still well

Georgia Camps 7 miles above dalton December 14th 1863
Dear beloved wife I again take my pen in hand to try to rite you a few lines to try to let you no that I am well and hope these few lines may find you all well and doing well I hant got but very little to rite to you we are here and have been 3 days but I dont think we will stay

138 See note to November 3.

here long our army is still folling back and the yankeys are advancing
slowly I dont no where we will make a stand at the most of our men
thinks we will fall back to atlanta georgia I think our cavalry is only
staying here to til the infantry gets out of the way Mariah I am sorry
to say to you that I am worse out of hart about whipping the yankeys
than I have every been there is lots of our men says there is no use to
fite them any more they say that bowth congresses has met[139] and I
hope they will make peace on some sort of terms of peace so we can
come home and live as we have done before it ant worth while to try
to tell how bad I want to come home I am afraid from what you rote
in your last letter that you and little geney is borth sick I would love
to here that you were all well one time more I want you to take good
care your self and the children and I will come home as soon as I can
I thought that asa would have started home before now on his detail
but I think it is a little uncertain whether he gets it or not there has
been several details sent but none of them hant come back yet you
said that Dave martin Jim Medill and coker was going to start here
the last of last month but they hant got here yet if they come here and
hant been mustered in to the service I will try to put one of them in as
a recruit and try to get a furlow Asa went out with a scout day before
yesterday and they cought a yankey and brought him in yesterday
morning if I could see you I could tell you a heap that I have seen
since I left home nothing more at present I remain your true devoted
husband til death   John W Cotton   I want you to hire manuel and
let him cost what he will

Georgia Camps 10 miles above dalton the 22 december 1863
dear wife I again embrace the opportunity of riting you a few lines
to try to let you no that I am well and hope these lines may find you
all enjoying the same blessing dave martin and bill got her nite before
last they brought me a letter and two par of socks and a bottle but no
brandy they said it all leaked out I was glad to here that your stock
was doing well I hope that you will have meat enough to do you I
cant rite but little now they have just brought in a yankey that one
picket captured last nite or this morning and I have got to go and
take him to headquarters he says the yankeys is all going back to chattanooga and are going to go down the river to rome and from there to
atlanta he come over to give up to us he is barefooted and nearly
naked he is from new yor city ases detail hant come back yet I am

139 Congress of the Confederate States was in session but there is nothing in the
Journal to indicate terms of peace were considered.

going to try to get a furlow on dave martin you sent me close enough
I had just drawed a very good pare of pants and could have drawn
more close if I had needed them I did not need the coks you sent to
me but I can keep them til I do need them I hope you will get manuel
next year from what dave martin says there wont bee no chance for
you to by him dave said pars stillhouse was burnt up and there wernt
but 10 stands saved but he did not no whether mine were burnt up or
not I would like to no we are all of our regiment on picket and I
expect we will bee here several days there is a heap of our cavalry gone
down below rome but we always have the blunt to have my horse has
been barefooted and I have had a heap of riding to do and he has fell
off a rite smart but I got him shod this morning we hant been geting
near enough for them to eat but we get a rite smart corn but no ruffage
our horses generally looks very bad and the most of them barefooted
I think I will bring or send my horse home and ride my mule I would
like to bee at home and help you pick spareribs and Carasus nothing
more at present I remain your true devoted husband til death John W.
Cotton

Georgia Camps 10 miles North of dalton december the 30. 1863
dear beloved wife I again take my pen in hand to rite you a few lines
to try to let you no that I am well and doing very well but I am sorry
to say to you that I have had very bad luck I have lost my horse he
dyed yesterday morning he dyed with the scours I done everything
for him I could but it done no good he was taken about midnite and
dyed nex morning we had started to charleston tennessee to try to
capture some yankey wagon trains and we staid all nite clost to cleve
land and 27 of us were put out on picket and the hole command went
on next morning and left us on picket and we stayed there all day in
3 miles of the yankeys and the rest of the command went on to
charleston and the wagon train had crossed the hiwassa river and some
of our men went up and skirmished with them some hour and a half
and were in the act of leaving and the yankeys made a charge on
them and stampeded the hole of our command and taken a heap of
them prisoners a killed some they run rite in to our men with their
pistols and sabers and shot and cut them with there sabers one struck
asa on the head with his saber but did not cut him very bad he got
away from them there is only one of our company missing lieutenant
guthry has not been herd of yet I escaped a scouring by beeing left on
picket we had 3 briggades in the stampeed there was several of our
boys lost there hats and nearly all of them lost there guns asa lost his

hat and bill martin and several others asa hant got his detail yet nor none of our company but there is lots of the regiment is gone home on details our boys sent them up and they wernt forwarded threw and they will have to send them up again I have sent up my furlow but it hant had time to come back yet nor I dont recken it will that stampeed I think will nock it in the head it is said our briggade will go down in alabama in a few days to decater but I am afraid we wont go I hope you have hired manuel before now and I hope these few lines may find you all well and doing well nothing more at present I remain your affectionate husband til death John W. Cotton

1864

Alabama Calhoun County January the 20 1864

Mariah dear wife I again take my pen in hand to try to let you no that I am well and where I am we are in allabamma 21 miles above talledega town we are gong to stop 6 miles below here at a place called the cold water campground and we have come down here to recruit our horses it is thought that we will stay down here about 2 months you may look for me at home before we go back to tennessee I rote to you that I had sent up a furlow I have not herd from it yet some that was sent up at the same time has come back disapproved and I have no idea that mine will ever come back I am going to try for another I think they will furlow all of us before we go back the dismounted part of our regiment hant got here yet asa is with them I reckon he has rote since I have I hant had the chance to rite in about 3 weeks we were on picket 8 days and when we were called off we started down here the next morning and tis is 10 days since we started our hole briggade is here 4 regiments I herd you had hired manuel again and had to give 150 bushels[140] of corn for him mis brown rote it to him I hant got a letter from you since dave martn came here I am anxious to here from you all but had rather see you all than here from you I am comeing home before I go back let cuts go as they will I rote to you that I had lost my horse I have got the mule that I captured yet but have hurt his back very bad on this trip if I get to come home I will bring him home I hant got but little to rite to you but if I could see you I could tell you a heap nothing more at present I remain your true affectionate husband til death
John W. Cotton

Oxford Alabama January the 24. 1864

Dear wife again take my pen in hand to rite you a few more lines to let you no that I am still well and hope these few lines may soon come to hand and find you the same. I will sent this to talladega by Wooderd Clare when you rite to me direct your letter to Oxford Alabama I rote to you the other day and I think I forgot to tell you where to direct your letters to I hant got a letter from you since dave martin left home nor asa neither I begin to want to here from you all very

---

[140] This is the only indication of how much wages was paid for Manuel.

bad I have sent up another furlow I started it day before yesterday
if I get it I will bee at home before long I hant got but little to rite
you we are building winter quarters and we have a very strict camp
gard and five roll calls a day and as soon as we get our cabins built
they are going to drill us twice a day in infantry drill we are not allowed to go out of camps without a pass approval by the general or the
briggade officer of the day and we are not ever allowed to ride our
horses to water some of the boys are very much dissatisfyed but I think
they are doing perfectly rite for if they did not have tite rools some of
them would bee allways gone and they would all most tare up the
country we have got a new general and I think he is the best on we
have been under his name is humes[141] my mules back has been very
sore but it is mending very fast if I get my furlough I will ride him
home it is only 21 miles from here to talladega we have had some of
the coldest weather that I ever saw it turned cold a christmas and
stayed cold til a few days ago we have had a few days of very pretty
weather but I think it will rain again in a few days I want to come
home to see you all and see how manuel is getting on with his farm I
herd you had hired him again nothing more at present I remain your
true devoted husband til death John W. Cotton

Alabama Oxford February the 1 1864
My dear beloved wife I again take my pen in hand to rite you a few
lines to try to let you here from em I am well at this time and hope
these few lines may find you the same I thought I would have been
at home before now but my furlow has not come back yet it looks like
that when a furlough is sent up it never comes back there has been
a heap of furloughs and details sent up since we come here but none
of them hant come back yet there is several of the boys got passes for
48 hours and went home but I dont want to come home on that sort
of pass but if my fur lough dont soon come back I shall try to come
some way my mules back has got most well his is mending very fast if
I get to come home I want to bring him and leave him and by me a
horse asa and dave martin is going to try to get a pass and come
home tomorrow if they do I may send this by asa if he comes home you
will be apt to see him and he can tell you more than I can rite we
have got very good shantys built and are doing very well we have to
drill twice a day and have 5 roll calls and are not allowed to go out

141 Brigadier-General W. Y. C. Humes of Tennessee rose from a lieutenant in the
cavalry.

of camps without a pass approved by the briggad officer of the day and are not allowed to ride a horse out of camp without a pass approved by general humes if I could see you I could tell you a heap I may get home before you get this letter and I may not come in some time I am looking for my furlough everyday I have to 2 letters from you since I rote before the last was rote the 10 th January I was sorry to here you had to give so much for the hire of manuel but I recken it is better to give that than to do worse your hogs done better than I expected nothing mor at present I remain your forever

John W. Cotton

Tumel hill Georgia March the 7. 1864
Dear wife and children I arrived here last nite at tumehill we brought 16 prisoners through with us we had a very wet mudy time of it but got along very well   there is a heap of duty to do here but the boys seem to bee in good sperite they say they are living better here than they did at oxford   beef has played out here and they draw bacon altogether I am on camp gard today lieute nant canant is in command of our company and he is on picket about 20 miles from here and they dont no when he will bee back he has been gone 12 days 10 of our company is with him we cant send up our furloughs til we see him I will go or send send to him this evening or tomorrow and have our furloughs filled up they are looking for a fite here before long if it stays good weather our men and the yankeys are picketing clost together they have some picket fiting once and a while there is a talk of our briggad going back to Oxford to recruit there horses again they say that it only takes a furlough 3 or 4 days to come back after it is sent up from here I weill get mine as soon as possible these lines leave me well and hopeing these few lines may come to hand and find you the same nothing more at present I remain your true devoted husband til death   John W. Cotton   Jim Brady has runaway and it s thought that he is gone to the yankeys

Oxford Alabama March 30th 1864[142]
Dear beloved wife I again take my pen in hand to try to let you no that I am at oxford yet but I recken we will leave here in the morning there is a parsel of the horses to the front we would have been gone before now but the commander here wouldent let us go by our selves I havent any thing to rite to you only to let you no that I am well and

---

[142] Cotton must have had a furlough here somewhere, for the tone of these two letters in March is more contented than earlier. See his comment on May 3.

all of the rest is well some of our boys that that was dismounted got
here last nite from dalton they say there is no fiting there but they
had orders to have all of there horses shod and have an extry pare to
take with them but they did not no where they were going but it was
thought they were going to make a rade some where nothing more I
remain yours forever   John W Cotton

Tunnel hill Ga.   aprile 23th 1864
Most dear beloved wife and children I take my pen in hand to try to
rite you a few lines to let you no that I am well in body but not in
mind I am very much troubled about not getting my furlough   Dave
Martin and bill got there furlough and started home yesterday evening I never have had nothing to hurt my feelings as bad in my life
general Johnson[143] has passed order for no more furloughs to be
granted for the present so there ant no chance now to get a furlough
I would give anything in the world almost to bee at home with you
now but as long as I cant my prare is that you may do well in deliver-
ing your der little babe do the best you can and take good care of
your self and the baby I dont no that I will ever live to see it but I
still live in hopes that I will live til the war will end so we can live in
peace and harmony once more I think if this war was ended I would
bee the happiest man living we are looking for a fite here every day
some of our regiment is gone now to run in some of the yankey pickets one of our men that went with them has just got in he says they
got 23 prisoners and killed 10 or 12 they are all comeing in we never
got nary man killed and but 2 wounded rite as soon as you get this
letter and let me no how you are comeing on and how manuel is getting on with his crop and how your wheat looks nothing more at
present I   remain your true devoted husband til death
                                            John W. Cotton

Tunnelhill Ga Aprile 28th 1864 Most dear wife and Children I once
more take my pen in hand to try to rite you a few lines to let you no
that I am well and hope these few lines may find you all the same I
want to here from you very bad I hant herd from home since Asa left
there I hope I will hear from you in a few days if ever we are looking

---

143 General Braxton Bragg had resigned his position as commanding officer in
the Army of Tennessee on December 1; on December 27 Joseph E. Johnston took
command. (Horn, *Army of Tennessee,* 305-320; *Official Records,* I, II, Part 2, Don
C. Seitz, *Braxton Bragg, General of the Confederacy,* Columbia, S. C.   The State
Company, 1924, chapter XI.) Seitz quotes lengthily from the Official Records.

for a fite here every day it would not surprise me to here at any minute that the yankeys wer advanceing general Johnson is moveing up
his force to the front it is said that he is mity well fortifyed betwixt
tunnelhill and dalton it is though that we will whip the yankeys here
our men seam to bee in good spirits and willing to fite[144] our cavalry
is in very good condition for fiting I am not satisfyed about my loose-
ing my furlough yet if I had got my furlough I mite have missed this
fite but I hope I will come out unhurt and live to see the war ended
and get home to enjoy the fruits of any labor here in this unjust and
unholy mess I dont no what I would give to bee at home with you and
our little ones but I cant bee with you now that 17 alabama regiment
is at rome ga but I recken you have herd from that there will be a
good deal of fruit in this country if nothing happens to it we had
frost here up to the 20 of this month but the weather is very warm
now and looks like spring has opened vegetation is putting forth very
fast nothing more at present that I can think of Asa is well and so is
porter asa is riting I hope these lines may find you all well   John
W Cotton

Tunnelhill Ga May 3th 1864
Most dear beloved wife and children I now take the opportunity to
rite you a few lines to let you no that I am still alive and well and
hope these few lines may find you all enjoying the same good blessing
we have had two little fites here since I rote to you before one the
next day after I rote and one yesterday but there wernt much damage
done yesterday morning the yankey run in our pickets on the ringgold
road and general humeses briggade met them and shermished with
them a while but there were such a heavy force of them that he fell
back below tunnel hill they com up near enough to throw some shells
to tunnel hill they threw also a few shells in to town and then fell
back our pickets were all called in and a regular fite were expected
but they went back all is quiet this morning so fare it is thought by
some that there would not bee no regular fite here soon it is believed
that they are sending there troops to verginia and trying to keep it
dark from us by showing fite here it is reported in camps that general
Johnson is sending troops from here to verginia it dont surprise me

---

144 A young officer wrote his wife, "I doubt if a volunteer army could be more
perfect in organization than the Army of Tennessee. General Johnston seems to
have infused a new spirit into the whole mass and out of chaos brought order and
beauty." (quoted in Horn, *Army of Tennessee,* 312). Other correspondence further confirm the fact that the morale of the army was high.

at no time now to here that the yankeys is coming for I am looking
for them every morning I thought that spring had come a few days
ago but we had a white frost last nite I dont think that is done much
damage I dont think it was cold enough to kill wheat nor frost much
but it killed the bushes rite smart in low places I recken Dave martin
and bill is setting up at home now digging (?) a grand rascal where
I would have been if I had got my rites I am not satisfyed about it yet
nor I never expect to bee I want to see you all very bad and I am
anxious to get a letter from home for I hant got nary one since I left
home but I hope you are doing well I would like to bee at home now
to see how manuel is getting on with his crop rite as soon as you get
these few lines and tell me if vardaman has fixed up my still nothing
more at present I remain your true affectionate friend til death

John W. Cotton

Hitower river near carters ville May 21th 1864
Most dear beloved wife I one time more take my pen in hand to try
to rite you a few lines to let you no where I am and what I am doing
I am not very well at this time I have been rite sick but I am mending
I will soon bee will I hope these few lines may find you all well and
doing well I got a letter from you dated the 7 of this month you said
that Sweat and giney were bowth sick I was very sorry to here that but
I was glad to here you was doing well and the baby[145] also you said
you wanted me to send it a name I hant got nary name picked out for
it if you have any one for it name it and I will be satisfyed with it I
dont no what to rite to you about the fite I no you have herd that we
were falling back we have fell back to the South side of hitower river
and give up all north of this river and we are still falling
back I dont no when we will make at stand at but general Johnston determed to fite them some where he has been trying to get them to fite him now for 2 weaks but they wont do it
they keep flanking him and he is oblige to fall back to keep them from
cutting him off from his supplies there has been a rite smart fiting but
no regular engagement[146] I think that we will whip them yet as soon
as we can get them to fite us it is thought that Johnson is getting
rinforcements from verginea he has got a very good army here now and

145 James Weaver Cotton was born April 28, 1864 (family Bible). He was known
to his family as Jim. He married Miss Jinnie White from Coosa County and later
moved to Waco, Texas. He lived until 1930. Mrs. Jeff (Nannie) Cotton, June
10, 1950).
146 Johnston's Fabian tactics in this area aroused great protest from **Richmond**.

they want to fite the infantry were the keenest for a fite at resacker[147] that ever I saw there is a heap of our men thinks we are whiped because we have fell back as for my part I hate very much haveing to give up so much of our own cuntry to the enemy to bee destroyed by them it makes me shudder when I think of the poor women and children that is left behind us the worst site that ever I saw is to see women and children running and hiding to keep beeing killed on the battle field since this fite has commenced I have seen them have to run from under the mouth of the cannon to keep from beeing killed you may think that you have some idea about it but you have none if I could see you now I could tell you a heap but I dont no whether I can send this letter off soon or not I hant rote in since the fite commenced for I hant had the chance to send letters off I got my horse shot the first day of the fite and I thought at first it would kill him but he has got nearly well he was not able for duty for a weak it has beeen done two weaks today he is doing very well he is a heap better horse than I though he was the yankeys had like to goot me when they shot my horse but I have escaped so fare there has been several of our company wounded slitely John Brady was wounded tolerable bad he is the only one gone to the horsepital nothing more I will again as soon as I get the chance may god bless you all nothing more

John W Cotton

Tunnelhill Ga May 26th 1864
Dear wife I take my pen in hand once more to try to let you here from me I am well and hope these few lines may find you all the same I hant but little to rite to you but I suppose you want to here whether we are fiting or not we are not at it yet but are expecting an attact every moment the yankeys are advancing on us they are not fare from tunnel hill in a line of battle we were saddled this morning by day and formed a line of battle and then marched to camps and not allowed to unsaddle we have had and allarm every day for several run out in a line of battle the men are getting so they dont care but very little for and allarm but I think if things dont change we will have something to do before sunday nite this friday morning our men are in good spirits it is generally believed that if they move on us here that we will whip them I here that the infantry is very anxious for a fite Asa is going now on a scout to see if the yankey are advencing and find out what they can there is fore others with him if I could

147 Resaca, Georgia.

see you I could tell you aheap that has passed since I come back to the company I dread this fite for I think the cavalry will have a heap to do and I dont no whether I will ever get out of it or not but I only have to trust to him who runs all things for my safety I hope he wil gide me safe threw the storms of battle and then return me safe home to you and our dear little ones[148] I hant got nary letter from you yet but asa got one from nan dated the 29 aprile she said you were still up and well rite and let me no how you are getting on nothing more at present John W. Cotton

May 27th 1864 Mariah dear wife I again take the privilege to rite you a few lines to try to let you no that I have just got two letters from you one was date may the 10 one the 17 I was glad to here that the children was all well and that you were don as well as what you were but sorry to here that your back hurt you so much I thank you for your prares and hope they may bee herd and granted Mariah we are still fiting the yankeys I am now riting clost to where they are fiting our briggade is now in a line of battle on the rite wing[149] of the infantry to keep off flankers the infantry are skirmishing and canonaiding very heavy there is a big fite expected here today we are 19 miles west of merietta ga there was a very heavy fite here day befor yesterday and heavy skirmishing yesterday our men whiped the yankeys very bad and tuck about 300 prisoners our briggade went on a raid last tuesday in rear of the yankeys and we captured there wagon train of over a hundred wagons and 20 days rashon for a hole division of ther armey and about 200 prisoners and several negros and 800 mules and 10 ambulanches and a car and two many things to mention our regiment received but little of the benefit of it for we were sent ten miles further in the rear to capture a train of cars but we never got to the railroad in time it had passed before we got there we passed clost by uncel travis Cottons[150] but I could not stop to see him I was with

148 This is one of the few references to religion.
149 General John B. Hood was over the right wing.
150 Travis Cotton was a brother of Cary Cotton. (*Deed Book* E. Coweta County, p. 72).
  Other brothers were Henry and Eli. At least one brother was dead for he left two minors, Bennett Cotton and Weaver Cotton. There were at least four girls in that family for in the settlement of the Weaver Cotton estate four men signed for their wives; William Hindsman (who married Nancy Cotton, the parents of Mariah Cotton), William B. Evans, Michael Hindsman, Micajah Bennett. Many of these were long lived people. Cary Cotton's tombstone shows he lived to be 79 and his wife 88; William Hindsman, "Uncle Billy," 83 "A notable pioneer and sterling citizen" (*Chronicles of Coweta County,* 237); Eli was also 83 (*Chronicles of Coweta*

the 1 georgia regiment day before yesterday all of our connection was
werl they told me that mike was maried to one miss turnett[151] I never
herd her name you may have herd of it before now dock is an as-
sistent surgeon in a horsepital at newnans they are bouth out of this
war I would like very much to see your big boy you rite so much about
Mariah I am sorry to say to you that I am not well for I am afraid you
will bee uneasy bout me but you need not I am able to go with the
company but not able to do much I have been unwell for two weaks
and have eat very little so my flesh is reduced rite smartly and
strenght two but I feel better today our regiment is allmost run down
there is lots of our horses runndown and gone to convalessent camps
and the men are all nearly wore out if I could get a few days rest I
think I would bee all rite but the other day when we made that raid
we started one nite about midnite and rode all that day and nite til
three oclock the next morning and there was one of the hardest rains
I ever saw and it was so dark I could not see my hand before me only
when it would liten so we have to travel some nearly every nite our
regiment has distinguished herself in this fite general wheeler[152] says
she is the best fiting regiment in his core we hant had many man killed yet but several wounded but all slitely but john brady he was
wounded in the back there has been several killed out of our regiment
nothing more at present I remain your fond affectionate husband til
death John W. Cotton Direct your next letter to merietta ga and I
will get it it will bee apt to follow us up

Coweta Co Ga 1864 May the 29
Dear Sister I will seat myself to write you a few lines to receive your
letter last week I was glad to herr from you this leaves us all well I
have nothing interesting to write at this time their is a grate excitement her about the yankee their was a faust alarm giving here last
week that they would be at Newnan thursday by twelve the people
was very excited here Sister you said that you want to no where Bud[153]
and Mike was Mike is at Aunt Kizy he is married he was married the

---

Co., 253). Not directly connected with the Cotton family but a brother of William
Hindsman was Israel Hindsman who lived to be 81 (*Chronicles,* 104).

[151] She must have lived out of Coweta County for the marriage is not recorded
there.

[152] Gen. Joseph Wheeler. A highly colorful biography of this Cavalry leader is
John Witherspoon DuBose's *General Joseph Wheeler and The Army of Tennessee*
(New York: The Neale Publishing Co., 1912) and in spite of its slightly sensational
style, the author quotes long passages from primary sources.

[153] This is the family name of Dr. A. C. L. Hindsman.

17 April to Emoline Tricit[154] Bud is at Andersonville he is a doctor
in the horsepittle[155]   Liz started their last sadurday was a weak ago I
dont no when whe will come back she went to carry some clothes to
him Sister I have not got any letter from John sence the fight he was
there at the fight but he was not hurt the last I herrd from him their
was one of his company killed and one got his leg shot off I dont
recond you would know them if I would name them Peter Hindsman
and Poke is in John Company Ben is at home all of the connection
is well except Aunt Sally and Uncle Israel they have the measels   I
must come to close Write soon   Nothing more remain yours truly Sister Nan Trammell[156]

Georgia June 1th 1864 Most dear beloved wife I once more take my
pen in hand to try to rite you a few lines to let you no where I am
and what I am doing and that I am about well and hope these few
lines may find you all well and doing well I have not received nary
letter from you since I rote I want to here from you very bad I want
to see you you dont no how bad it ant no use to try to tell anything
about it but there ant no chance to come home now our cavalry is
doing more now than they have since the war begun Wheelers cavalry
is on the rite wing of our armey and they are lying in line of battle
tide infantry we have built splendid breastworks and are ready for and
attact we keep our horses about one mile in the rear and 1 man to
ever 4 horses to attend to them and the rest at the brest works and on
the sherman line the skermishes fite day and nite but they are so fare
a part there ant but very little damage done I rote to you once since
we have been here I rote that we were looking for a heavy fite there
was a rite smart fite that evening our briggade was in it but they did

---

154 The names given by Cotton and Mrs. Trammell hardly coincide.

155 Andersonville, Georgia, was the Confederate prisoner-of-war hospital which is
one of the prisons that has colored public opinion. Two sympathetic studies, the
first from the North and the other from the South are James Madison Page, *The
True Story of Andersonville Prison*, (New York: The Neale Publishing Co. 1908) ;
and R. Randolph Stevenson, *The Southern Side; or Andersonville Prison*, (Balti-
more: Turnbull Brothers, 1876.) The author of the last book was at one time chief
surgeon of the Confederate States Military Prison Hospitals at Andersonville. Coulter says of the Page book "the book is a valuable contribution to an understanding
of prison life in the Confederacy and is unique among prisoner-of-war accounts
because it defends the Confederate prison regime" (E. Merton Coulter, *Travel in
the Confederate States, Bibliography*, Norman: University of Oklahoma Press, 1948
p. 197). Checking through this bibliography reveals few other accounts that are
not bitterly biased.

156 Nancy Hindsman Trammell, sister of Mariah Cotton.

not fite long til the infantry came in and releaved them our majoy got his arm shot off at his shoulder and another private shot threw the rist and several slitely wounded but nary one killed nor nary one of our company wounded we have had 8 of our company wounded since this fite commenced but nary one killed but there has bee several of the regiment killed me nor Asa hant been touched asa is well he has been in to the fite all the time my horse has got well and is doing well hes wound did not hurt him as bad as I thought it would the ball went in at the bulge of his ribs and come out near his sheath and out the skin on his thy they were shooting mity clost at me there has been several rite hard fites here since we have been here and our men have wiped them in every instance[157] and there loss has been very heavy this eavning our briggade was in to it our loss were 50 killed and our men buryed 650 yankeys besides what they caried off our men whiped them and tuck the battle field we have not had no general engagements yet but we are looking for it every day but a heap thinks the yankeys wont come on us but I think if they dont in a few days that Johnson will go on them they have been trying to flank us on the rite but they have failed so fare I think if they will come up and fite us that we will whip them badly this is enough about the fite I would like to bee at home to see how you all are comeing on and how manuel is getting on with his crop I wish vardaman would fix up my still if there is fruit enough to still if you get the chance send vardaman word to come and fix it up if par wants to fix it up and still on it let him have it for half he makes and you may let manuel help him when he has time you must name the baby and send me its name nothing more at present only I remain your true deveoted husband til death John W. Cotton

Georgia Camps 5 miles north of merietta June 9th 1864 Dear beloved wife I again take my pen in hand to try to rite you a few lines to let you no that I am well and hope that you are enjoying the same blessing I want to here from you very bad I hant got nary letter from you since the 17 of last month we get but very littel mail there is but very few letters comes to our company I am afraid you dont get mine for I no you want to here what we are doing up here the big fite hant come

---

[157] A day by day account, taken largely from General Sherman's reports, can be found in W. D. Dodson (ed.), *Campaigns of Wheeler and His Cavalry* (Atlanta: Georgia, 1899). A more recent biography of Wheeler is John P. Dyer *"Fightin Joe" Wheeler*, (Baton Rouge: the Louisiana State University Press, 1941). The author, in Chapter VII "The Atlanta Campaign", goes into some detail of these activities.

off yet the yankeys are trying to flank us yet on the rite but I think
they have gone about as fur as they can go our briggade is picketing
on the left there is but very few yankeys where we are picketing we
hant done any fiting now is six days and there has not bee but little
fiting on the lines the yankeys charged our men nite before last at
bug shanty and we killed and captured fif teen hundred of them that
is about the way they get done every time they attact us I think if
they would come up and fite us a fare fite that we would give them
the worst whipping they ever got it is reported by deserters and citizens comeing in to our lines that they are suffering very much for the
want of rashons and that there horses and mules are starving for want
of forage from all accounts there armey is in a very bad condition[158]
our armey is in good spirits and are getting a plenty to eat our horse
rashons are short we dont get but half rashons of corn but we get
green wheat to feed on our horses have stood up very well considering
what they have had to do I want to see the baby very bad and all the
rest of you nothing more at present I remain your as ever
                                                    John W. Cotton

Camps near Merietta June 17th 1864
Dear beloved wife I take my pen in hand to rite you a few lines to try
to let you no that I am well and hope these few lines may find you
enjoying the same blessing I got a letter from you sent by dave martin you said you did not get my letters I was sorry to here that for I
no that you want to here from me while this fight is going on here I
hant been hurt yet we had another fite day before yesterday we got
our orderly sargent killed he was all that got hurt out of our company
there was two killed and one wounded in our regiment we made the
yanks get back they are fiting every day some where on the line but
there hant been no regular fite yet but we are looking for it every day
we have had a heap of rain and the roads have been very muddy but

---

158 To Southerners who have been reared on the theory that the Civil War was
lost because the Union was superior in material goods, statements like this come
as a surprise. It is a matter of fact, of course, that neither side had a good system
of supply. A fresh source on the Union side has turned up recently in the Osborne
Manuscript owned by Mrs. Murray Flynn in Montevallo, Alabama. V. B. Osborne,
an enlisted man in the 2nd Kansas Cavalry, fought for four years in the South-West,
chiefly in S. W. Missouri and Arkansas. He tells about guns but no bullets, saddles
but no horses, days with no supplies and frequent times when the only food was
apples pilfered from orchards in the region, etc. His outfit was never issued any
clothes except shirts and socks. This manuscript is being published in the *Kansas
Historical Quarterly*, edited by Joyce Farlow.

they are getting better the yanks have quit trying to flank us I think
that they have got where they will have to fite or back out I think if
they come on to our men in there brest works I think they will get a
good whipping but I dont think that general Johnson will go on them
I hant got but little to rite to you I hant got nary letter from you by
mail since the 17 of may I no it ant because you dont start them I
want to see you very bad and I want to see that big boy and see how
he looks I hant got no name for him yet I want you to name him and
send me his name I hope you will get these lines in dieu time and I
hope they may find you well and doing well nothing more at present
I remain your true devoted friend til death

John W Cotton

Georgia Camps 4 miles west of Merietta June 22nd 1864 Most dear
beloved wife I once more take my pen in hand to try to let you here
from me and to answer your kind letter of June 10th I was glad to
here the children was all well but sorry to here you were pestered so
bad with the spring nettles but it may keep you from beeing sick otherwise[159] I begin to want to see that big boy of yourn that you brag
on so much and I am anzious to see all of the rest of you I tryed to
swap my horse for a 15 days detail to come home but my officers
woundent let me do it there is five of my company gone home now on
details and there is one here for william lessley but he is gone to the
horsepital he was very [sick] and had the shingles very bad it was cold
that rilled him we have the most rain here that ever I saw it is all
most impossible to ride the roads in places I think that is keeping off
a general fite the roads in places I think that is fiting here every day
and some days very heavy our regiment hant been in a fite since se-
bron Johnson was killed he was the man our briggade was in a fite
day befor yesterday but our regiment was sent around on the left to
stop a rode of yankeys but they went back and we are here yet on
the left of our enemy we have been on the rite all the time no more
about the fite these lines leave me well you said you new that we lived
hard in this fite but you are mistaken if you could see the pork that
we eat yesterday and this morning our bread baked and brought to
us and we have been drawing ½ pound of bacon a day I cant let ould
man holingshead have that iron I never got lises letter in yourn like

---

[159] There was a folk saying "a boil was worth a spell of sickness." It was com-
monly believed even much later than this that any kind of a "breaking out" or rash
would prevent an illness.

you will make a good crop of wheat dont bee uneasy about me I will
do the best I can I hope that your prayers may bee answered nothing
mor at present I remain your John W Cotton your pen ant no worse
than mine

Marietta Ga June 27th 1864
My most dear beloved wife I take my pen in hand to try to rite you a
few lines in ancer to your kind letter I received from you last nite
dated June the 16 I was very glad to get it and to here that you were
all well and all of the connections these here lines leave me well and
hoping they may find you the same I am at in in the country 3 miles
from camps having some close washed at 50 cts a garment and it only
half done at that you said you wanted to see me very bad I would bee
glad you could I want to come very bad but there aint no chance now
til this fite is over you rote to me some time ago that ould porter
vardermon and some body else had been talking about me I want you
to rite to me what they said and what it was you said you wanted to
me me if I wanted my still fixed up any how I do if you can get it done
if I can get get it fixed up I would rent it out if I could if there aint
fruit enought to still maybe some body mite want to make some whiskey have them stands maid up you can get it done I would like to no
how my mule is comeing on at ould man lessleys I want him to get
fat by the time I need him my horse looks very well yet and so does
ases the boys were all well this morning porter is gone to the horsepital I hant herd from him since he left there is a detail here for him
to go home after a horse if he gets a furlough from the horsepital tell
him I want to by it and for him to rite to me what he will take for it
[I saw] Coker the other day he said they were all well you said there
was a heap of talk of peace I had not herd anything of it up here nor
seen anything of it in the papers I dont want to kill your hopes for
peace but I dont see no chance for peace til we whip the yankees out
here and at richmond we were on the left of our enemy when I rote
to you before but we have come back to our briggade general allen[160]
has quit us colonel anderson[161] is in command of our briggade we hant
had no fiting to do since I rote before unless there has been some done
today a curier come to colonel andersons head quarters just before I
started out here and said the enemy were advanceing there has been
heavy canonaiding all along the lines today it is the heavyest that has

160 General W. W. Allen.
161 J. Patton Anderson.

been since the fite commenced but I dont no what has been done I
think it has been mostly artillery dweling I herd an ould citizen say
that he herd in merietta that general Johnson was a going to give
them a general fite this evening but there ant near as mauch canonaiding now as there has been all day it has nearly all ceased but it may
brake loose in one moment worse than ever it is now about 4 o'clock
I will start back to camp as soon as I get my letter done my pass it out
at seven oclock the yanks are still trying to flank to the left I think
we will whip them rite here is they dont flank us out of our positions
ours is a splendid position here we have the top of kennasin[162] mountain covered with art illery you out to see it turned loose at the yankeys nothing more
I remain your true devoted husband til death John W Cotton to his
dear wife at home

Camp near Chattahooche river July the 4 1864 Mariah dear wife I
again take my pen in hand to rite you a few lines to try to let you
no that I am well and still livin and I still hop these few lines may
reach you in dew time and find you all enjoying the same good
blessing Mariah I would like to see you to tell you some thing about
how we are getting along with the yankeys for I no I cant give you
much satisfaction about it by riting they have flanked us out of merietta at last they would not fite us at kannasaw mountain and kept
flanking to the left so we had to fall back between there and the river
and some think that we will fall back across the river before we can
make a successful stand for all we keep falling back we have hat a
heap of little fites with them and have killed and wounded a heap of
while our loss have been comparativerly small from there own accounts we have killed and wounded betwixt 50 and 75 thousand of
there men since we left tunnel hill[163] there is a rite smart bumming a
going on now on our left yesterday as we fell back our briggade got
in to a terrible shelling and several of our briggade got killed and
wounded but none of our company got hurt all of the neighbors boys
are well I hant herd from porter since he went to the horsepital I
have got 2 bunches of thread I whish you had they were going to burn
up some in merietta to keep the yankeys from getting it and the sol-

[162] Kenesaw Mountains.
[163] This is, of course, an exaggerated figure. It seems only estimates of the dead
here are available. Johnston said there were killed 9,972 in his command exclusive
of the cavalry and that the enemy dead were "six times as great". (Horn, *Army
of Tennessee*, 339).

diers tuck it nothing more we are ordered to saddle up and I cant rite
any more now may god bless you and protect you all   John W Cotton

Atlanta Ga August the 1. 1864[164]
dear beloved wife I once more take my pen in hand to rite you a few
more lines to try to let you no that I am well and have got to my command safe or to our wagon train I got her day before yesterday my
briggade is gone after a yankey rade and I here where they are the
raid they are after crossed the chattahooche river and burnt palmead-
ow and tore up the railroad the nite I staid at John Fulmers comeing
up her lots of the people run out of newman thinking they were
comeing there but they struck across towards griffin and tore up the
other road between atlanta and griffin there is a heap of our cavalry
after them and we here they have captured a heap of them I will start
to hunt them today or tomorrow it tuck me six days to get here I had
to go to westpoint to cross the river genral armstrong had sunk all the
flats aleone I came threw came to and saw a heap of connection I saw
auld John Israel Ben Crittyamm and sally Isarel at uncel mikes I
stoped there and got dinner uncle mike is gone to the war and uncle
isarel is stilling they are makeing a heap of brandy and selling it at
$100 per gallon I went from there to Johns and staid all nite I went
by aunt lizzes and your paps the connection is all well your brother
mike is gone to the war two they are takeing all of the detailed men
and putting them in the war John had to report to town as I came on
but I dont no what they done with him whether they will send him off
or not the hindsmands are mitely opposed to uncle mikes haveing to
go to the war I hant seen any of our settlement boys yet they are all
with the regiment I sent moses and to neys letters to them by one of
there briggade the rest of the letters I brought I have got yet there is a
bad chance to get them to the boys for there ant no postoffice now in
atlanta it is moved out and there ant no chance only to send them by
hand I would like to tell you a heap about there fiting up here but I
cant tell but little about it I here that they had a very hard fite for
her last friday was a weak ago and general hardea whiped the yankeys
and taken fore thousand prisoners and they had a fite with the cavalry
and John tramels company got badly cut up colonel strickland is

164 The letter from the Adjutant General says, "The Company muster roll for
May and June 1864, dated 30 June 1864, last on file, shows him absent with the
remark 'On furlough.'" (Edward F. Witsell, Adjutant General to Lucille Griffith,
April 5, 1950). There is some error some where because he wrote home during the
time. He was home, though, in July as is indicated by this letter.

wounded but no very bad and lish tramel is badly wounded threw the thy and several others you dont no and some killed and pete hindsman taken prisoner uncle john was takeing on very bad about it my regiment hant done any fiting since I left it unless they have fought that raid they are after they were a very heavy fite her last friday I was in hereing of it but I dont no the result but I herd that the yankeys charged the militia gave them a good whipping they got the railroad to macon done yesterday where the yankeys tore it up and sent off a load of wounded soldiers I swaped off my mare before I got up her and got one of the finest kind of mules for her it has been raining a rite smart since I left home and I am in hopes you have had rain since I left nothing more at present I remain your true devoted husband til death   John W Cotton

Georgia Camps three miles from the Social Circle on the Augusta railroad and fifty miles from Atlanta August 10th 1864
Most dear beloved wife   again I take my pen in hand to try to rite you a few lines to try to let you no that I am well and doing very well I hant any nuse to rite to you I recon Asa has rote to you about the rade that they were after when I got her we are fiting now to make a raid in rear of the yankeys   it is thought we will start tomorrow   I dont recon you will here from me any more til we come back if I ever come back I will rite again   I hope we will be able to pay them back for all the raids they have made on us if we can bee successful in getting in there rear and cut off there supplies it may bee the means of making them fall back from Atlanta   there has been two very hard fites here at Atlanta[165] since I left home and reports says our men whiped them badly   we still hold Atlanta and I hope we will bee able to still hold it   Mariah I hant seen Asa since I got here the rest of the boys says he stoped at his pars but he may be at home for what I no he has been gone over a weak I got a letter for him that nan sent by oneal and read it I was glad to here you were all well   it had a letter in it for tony   I mailed to him. Asa captured two yankey horses and

[165] Books on the Battle of Atlanta are numerous; in addition to those specifically about this battle, nearly every general involved has a biography which goes into varying detail about activities in the area. A few are Horn, *Army of Tennessee;* Du Bose, *General Joseph Wheeler and the Army of Tennessee;* Dyer, *Joseph Wheeler.* W. T. Sherman, *Personal Memoirs* (New York: Charles L. Webster and Co., 1890), John B. Hood, *Advance and Retreat* (New Orleans: 1880), Official Records XXXVIII, *Battles of Atlanta* prepared under the direction of the committee of the Atlanta Camp, Atlanta, 1895.

bridals   I hope these few lines may reach you in dieu time and find
you well and doing well it is uncertain whether you get this letter or
not but you may get it after while nothing more at present   I remain
your affectionate husband til death   John W Cotton

East tennessee Camp 4 miles from Jonesborough 100 miles north east
of noxville September 24th 64   My dear beloved wife it is with uncer-
tainty that I rite you a few lines you may get this and you may not but
I hope you will these lines leave me well this is the 45 day we have
been on this rade and I have been well all the time dont bee uneasy
about me we hant had but little fiting to do but I have been in it all
and hant been hurt yet I think we are out of danger now we are incide
of our own lines we have had three men captured on this trip Burten
Shaw and William Deason and a man by the name of Broice and one
wounded Porter and Brown is well and all of the company is well how
come us here we act behind general wheeler and got cut off from
him[166] there is a 2 briggades of us and a part of another our men were
very uneasy while we were in the yankey lines for fear we would bee
captured but we got out safe we whiped the yankeys where ever we
come in contact with them we have tore up a great deal of railroad on
our rout but I am afraid it hant done much good we here that the
yankeys has got atlanta[167] but I here that our men has taken it back
it ant worth while to say how bad I want to see you I hant here a
word from you since I left home and this is only the three letter I
have rote to you if I could see you I could tell you a heap I will rite
more as soon as I get the chance nothing mor I remain your true lover
til death   John W. Cotton

1864

October the 2 Mariah I will rite a few more lines as I have not had
the chance to send off my letter yet I am still well and hope these lines
may find you all well and doing well I hope ann is well by this time I

166 Wheeler, with 4,500 men, about half the Cavalry, was sent against the Western
and Atlantic railroad between Atlanta and Chattanooga in hopes to force Sherman
into retreat. After making demonstration around Marietta, Dalton and Chattanooga, "on some wild impulse" he rode through east Tennessee as far north as
Strawberry Plains above Knoxville. Federal troops were sent against them and both
Wheeler and Forrest were forced into North Alabama. (Horn, *The Army of Tennessee*, 363; Dyer, *Wheeler*, 189-196; Dodson, *Campaigns of Wheeler*, 248-273.)

167 Hood, who had assumed Command of the Army of Tennessee on July 17,
evacuated Atlanta on September 1.

saw oald anchy meneal about two weaks ago and he said he was at the
still and he never herd any complaint that is all that I have herd from
home since the 18 of august and I recken you no that I want to here
from home by this time we have had a powerful rain it rained a day
and two nites but it is the first rain we have had since I got back from
home except one little shour we have had the dustyest time that I ever
saw I have seen the dust so thick that I could not see no more than I
could the darkest kind of a nite it looked like it would stifle men and
horses on a march I hant seen asa in some time but I think I well see
him today I am going to the post office and they say our dismounted
men is camped clos to the post office and they say it is 7 miles from
here every thing is still here yet there is no fiting going on yet but I
am looking for it every day Meneal told me that the cavalry that were
hunting up deserters killed oald stephen thomas I was sorry to here of
it I dont no what else to rite nothing more I will rite again before
long

Camped near thomaston Ga November 24 1864 Dear beloved wife I
now take my pen in hand to rite you a few lines to let you no that I
am well and all the rest of the boys we are ordered to macon ga what
forces that are not with hood in tennessee are all reporting at macon
I recon you will here before you get this that the yankeys have burnt
atlanta and all left there they are not far from macon some where but
I cant tell you where it is thought they are trying to go to charleston
where or savannah Mariah I though I would get to go by your paps
but I never got the chance the nearest I got there was at greenville it
will take us two more days to go to macon I hant anything to rite at
present I will rite you again in a few days if I have the chance I hope
these few lines may find you all well direct your letters to macon
georgia nothing more but remain your best friend til death
John W Cotton

Camps Macon Ga November 26th 1864
Most Dear beloved wife I again take my pen in hand to try to let you
no that I am well and all of our boys are too we have got to macon
but the yankeys are gone they come near enough to throw shell in
macon but the malish kept them of they only sent there cavalry here
while there infantry passed on they are at miledgville or have been
for several days old shermans headquarters has been at miledgville it
is thought they are making for savannar they are followed clostly by
wheelers cavalry we will go on after them as soon as we can get arms

and equip ment there is a talk of our drawing money but that is uncertain the man I sold my horse to told me this morning that he was
ready to take up his note I have got my saddlebags and all my close
but my pants some damd theaf took them out of my saddle bags if I
ketch him with them on I will raise him out of his boots one time I
hant got anything worth riting nothing more at present only I remain
your true devoted husband til death

John W Cotton

Direct your letters to John W Cotton Co (C) 10 Confederate regt
Macon Ga they say we will draw close today and I will try to draw
some pants asa says tell his folks he is all a setting we have had some
very cold weather I wanted to come by your paps but I never got the
chance and didnot Dave martin sold his stolen horse that ant no account so he is about a foot again his ould horse give out and he got
15 days detail to go home to get another and dave has swindled him
out of it nothing more I will rite again when I get the chance
Camps on Conoochee river 22 miles west of Savannah December the
6th 1864 Dear beloved wife I again take my pen in hand to rite you a
few lines to let you no that I am well and not fare from savannah and
the yankeys a folowing us up we hant got to wheeler yet we have got
about 350 mane with us we have just got out of a pen we have just
crossed a little river and are just wating for the yankeys to come to
burn the bridge to keep them from crossing we come across some of
there mounted infantry and stempeeded and we run them about 7
miles and tuck 31 prisoners and several mules and horses and two negroes and lots of commissaries they had gethered up that day in the
neightborhood they were out a forageing for there armey we had the
field day before yesterday and yesterday we fooled along [   ] they
had like to go us hemed between [   ] rivers we had but one place to
cross so we started this morning before day and we have got out of
there way now if they dont get us hemed again we are not fare from
wheeler but we will have to go about sixtey miles to get to him it is
thought by a heap that the yankeys are not going to savannah but
leave it to there left and stricke the cost away below savannah they are
now in the poreest country I every saw it is a very porr flat pine cuntry from here to macon and the thinest settled cuntry I ever saw the
yankey are destroying everything before them and ravishing women
the citizens are fleeing from them like chaft before the wind If I could
see you I could tell you a heap about how they are treating citizens

and a heap other things two tedious to mention[168] I would like to here from you all and here how you are getting along and whether your hogs has tuck the colery or not nothing more at prseent I hope these few lines may find you all well and doing well   John W Cotton Direct your letter to savannah ga you ort to have seen them yankeys run til they got to there main armey and then they got behind there brest works and we let them alone and got away with our prisoners

Savannah Ga December 15th 1864
Most dear beloved wife I again take my pen in hand to try to let you no where I am and to let you no that I am well and hope these few lines may find you all well and doing well we are in side of the breast works at savannah the railroads are all cut between here and home so we cant send letters out by mail there is a negro a going to start to mongomery tomorrow so we will send our letters out by him he is going out horseback and he will mail them on the way we are looking for a fite here every day there is a rite smart skirmishing on the lines all the time and some times very heavy canonaiding the shell our lines but do but little damage one of our company got slitely wounded in the head today on the skirmishline his name is smith our boys are all well but porter he has been complaining of the toothache for several days there has come an order here today from general hardee for our horses to bee sent across savannah river til the fite is over and send one man to every three horses we are camped 8 miles from town but we staid in town one nite and I saw the city it is a fine town I would like to here from you I hant herd from you since I left home I would like to bee at home I want to come home very bad I hope it wont bee long before we can come home and stay there what is left of us the boys dont like the idea of beeing dismounted and I dislike it very much myself we have not go with wheeler yet they say that he is just on the other side of savannah river but they wont let us go to them we have been here 7 days there is not many places that the yankeys can come in to savannah with a force it is surrounded with some little rivers and big marshes on each side so it is impossible for them to cross they say we have fourteen thousand troops here it is thought that we will have to give up the by a great many but there is the gratest natural devence

[168] Most books about the battle of Atlanta also include Sherman's march through Georgia. Sherman's version of it is given in his *Personal Memoirs*, II, 171-267; the Confederate in *Confederate Military History* vol. VI and both sides in *Official Records*, Series 1, XLIV.

I ever saw they have taken one of our forts on the coast for McCalister
every thing is unusuall still this eavning I would like to here what
general hood is doing I dont get any nuse atall I am afraid it will be
a long time before I here from you and I am afraid you wont get this
letter this is the third time I have rote since I left home I rote sooner
but I saw no chance to send a letter off nothing more at present only
I remain your true devoted husband and friend til death
                         John W Cotton

Camps East of Savannah December   1864
Most dear beloved wife I once more take my pen in hand to try to rite
you a few lines to try to let you no that I am well and hope these few
lines may find you all well and doing well all of the boys are well so
fare as I no asa and porter is gone off with our horses I hant seen them
in several days I recken you have herd before now that our company
was dismounted in savannah and our horses sent I have rote to you
about it   I told asa to rite and I (   )169 when he has done it and he
had better chance to send off letters than I have had he has been 30
or 35 miles above here where had a better chance to send off letters
than I have we have evacuated savannah and are now on the east side
of savannah river and the yankeys are all on the west side of the river
all of our cavalry are leaving here but our briggade they say they are
ordered to tennessee and I dont think that we will stay here very long
I hant herd from home since I left you dont no how bad I want to
here from you all but I had rather see you all than to here from you
but there is no chance to see you I am very anxious to have [ ] of this
[ ] and unholy war ending so I can come home and all the rest of
the boys to live in peace with mankind I think if I was out of this
war I would bee the happiest man in america almost every bady thinks
the war will end soon but for my part I cant see no chance for it to end
unles we go back in to the union and free the negroes the yankeys
hant hurt eny thing in savannah so reports say they say there is a heap
of georgia stat [   ] that stayed in savannah when we crossed the
river [   ] are now staying with [   ] this christmas day but we hant
got anything to drink it very dull time here and it is with you to
drink [   ] eggnog for me as I cant get any here I would like to bee at
home to help you eat sawsedg and pick spare ribs and back bones if
you have had good luck with your hogs I would like to here whether
the colery got among your hogs or not and how things are in general

169 Manuscript illegible.

my mule is doing very well I am riting I dont no whether you will get this letter or not I have rote [?] times since [?] left home or not no more at present   John W Cotton[170]

Camp December 23th 1864 Dear beloved wife I take my pen in hand to try to let you no that I am well and hope these few lines may find you all well and doing well Savannah is evacuated and we have all got out safe we are now in southcarolina about six miles from savannah our company is all dismounted but three me and billy brown and sentel our horses are ordered back to the men they will bee here today or tomorrow there was some yankeys on this side of the river but they have all gone back on the other side the boys are all wll I hant got anything to rite I hant herd from home since I left home I dont no whether you will get this letter or not this is all nothing more at present I remain your true devoted husband til death   John W Cotton   Direct your letters to Charleston south carolina

Southcarolina camps nar Savannah December 30 1864
Dear beloved wife I take my pen in hand to rite you a few lines to let you no that I am still well and hope these few lines may find you all enjoying the same good blessing I hant got but little to rite you I rote you a letter a christmas day and I rote all the nuse that I had we are still picketing on Savannah river in site of savannah there has been no move here by the enemy since they got savannah I herd today that wheelers core was ordered to tennessee there is some of company A of our regiment going to start home tomorrow of furlough they have lost there horses since I left home but I dont no whether you have got any of them or not I hant herd from home since I left home want to here from home very bad they are fixing the payroles to draw money we will draw 8 months wages I got pay for my horse at macon there has been some picket fiting today across the river but no hurt done our side only two horses killed I dont think we will stay here much longer if we dont go to tennessee we will fell back out of this flat country it is very flat and marshy there ant anything raised here hardly but rice our cavalry is very much out of hart I can think of anything more to rite at present I remain your true devoted husband til death
John W Cotton

[170] This mouse eaten letter was more damaged than most of them.

1865

Camps January 9th 1865

Most dear beloved wife I once more take my pen in hand to try to rite you a few lines to try to let you no that I am well and hopeing these few lines may find you all the same I hant got any thing to rite to you only to try to let you no that I am well there ant eny thing new transpired since I rote before I hant got nary letter from you yet you dont no how bad I want to here from hom I would give any thing to bee at home and see you all and no how you are getting along I have rote several letters to you since I left home and I dont no whether you have got them or not we have not got any mail here since I left home only a few letter rote about the 15 of december we are now about 30 miles from savannah on the Augusta road the yankeys advanced on us and we fell back and bloccaded the road behind us they are not makeing any move now that I no of I here today that we are agoing to move up the country tomorrow to recruit our horses we will move towards augusta I think we will move if the yankeys dont make no move before we get off I will start this by one of our regiment that is going home dave martin hant got here yet he is droped from the roll they have just made out the paroles to draw money[171] and they have droped all from the roll that have been absent 7 days without leave there is several droped from the roll Bill Adkins is droped too nothing more at present only I remain your true affectionate friend til death   John W Cotton to his wife at home

South Carolina Camps near Lortonsville[172]   January 20th 1865

Most dear beloved wife I again take my pen in hand to rite you a few more lines to try to let you no that I am well and doing well all is quiet at the front now I have not herd any canonadeing for several days the yankeys have got pocalatize[173] that is on the railroad about halfway from savannah and charleson we have moved twice since I rote to you before we are now 75 miles from augusta we are getting a plenty to eat ourselves and our horses we are not doing anything but

---

171 The soldiers had not drawn any pay for ten months (*Official Records*, XXXVIII, Part r, 1027).

172 Search thus far has not revealed any such place. It may be Lawtonville which is named by Horn. The letter of February 1 may be dated from the same place.

173 Pocotaligo.

recruiting our horses my mules is fatter than he was when I left home
we have five roll calls a day and I drill and dress peraid we have not
drawn our money yet but I have plenty I would like to send you some
for I am afraid you hant got money enough to pay your war tax but
this ant what bothers me most I ant herd from you since I left home
but I hope you have herd from me if I cant from you you cant no
how bad I want to here from home asa got a letter from you the
other day but nan never said anything about you all but I reckon you
were all well or else would have said so Mr. brown has got two letters
from home and I dont see why I dont get none from you I no you
must rite I would rote this time but I thought I mite get a letter from
you I will start this by hand as there is no regular mail from here I
hant any nuse we here the general hood is whiped out of tennessee
and is in Mississippi[174] and we here that a part of lees armey is at
branchville southcarolina it looks like the yankeys has got the upper-
hand of us I would like to here of some terms of peace before the runn
clear over us I think they will take charlestan without a fite our soldiers are very much dishartened and the most of them say we are
whiped it is said that georgia is holding conventions to no whether to
go back in the union or not if she goes back it will look like rest will
have to go two I hate the thoughts of going back but if we have to do
it the sooner the better I have suffered two much in this war to ever go
back to the union willingly I would give a heap of see you and the
children and see you all well and have one frolick with them there is
nothing in this world that can gratify my feelings like beeing with a
kind and affectionate wife I dont think that if I were at home to stay
clere of this war I would ever want to leave home again hothing more
at present only I remain affectionate husband til death   John W
Cotton

[174] Following the fall of Atlanta there was so much criticism of Hood that it
became necessary to make some changes. Hood kept his position with the Army of
Tennessee but a new unit, the "Military Division of the West" embracing the commands of Hood and General Richard Taylor was created and placed under the
Command of General Pierre G. T. Beauregard. No one seems to know who origi-
nated the idea for Hood to take the Army of Tennessee into Tennessee but Sherman knew about it from the speeches of President Davis as reported in the Confederate newspapers. Hood's task seems to have been to destroy railroads and
thereby cut Sherman's line of supply and communication. After much confusion,
angry disputes as to responsibility and crushing defeats at Franklin and Nashville,
Hoods army rested for a short time at Tupelo, Mississippi (Horn, *Army of Tennessee*, 394-422; Thomas Robson Hay, *Hood's Tennessee Campaign*, New York:
Walter Neale, 1929).

January 23, 1865 Dear wife I will rite you a few more lines my letter
is not gone yet the man I gave this letter did not start when he promised to so I will send it by another man that says he will start tomorrow morning these few lines leave us all well I am well and all of our
boys there is nothing new happened since I rote we have had a heap
of rain and our camps are very mudy it has been raining 4 days and
the place where we are camped is so flat the water dont run off this
is a very flat marshy cuntry any how but not as bad as it is down about
savannah the roads are very sandy they dont get mudy here like they
do in tennessee the people here are generaly rich and they are all
refugeeing it looks now like it would clear off mr brown is riting and
asa will send a few lines in with one I hant got but little to rite but I
think if I could get a leter from you to answer I could rite a heap
more maby you dont direct you letters rite direct the next to John
W. Cotton Augusta G. Andersons briggade 10 Confederate regt Co
(C) I have looked for a leter til I have nearly give it out it looks like I
wont get nary other letter at all but if I cant get yours I hope you will
get mine and I hope they may find you all well and doing well dave
martin hant got here yet I rote you that he was droped from the roll
but he is not the lieutenant had orders to do it but he never did it we
hant drawn money yet I would love to no whether ould man brown
has got his corn yet or not and how ould manuel is geting on with
the farm and how your fatning hogs turned out and how you all are
getting along nothing more I hope to get a letter from you soon   John
W. Cotton

Camp Southcarolina January 27th 1865
Most dear beloved wife and hyly esteemed wife   I once more take my
pen in hand to rite you a few more lines to try to let you no that I am
well and in hopes these few lines may find you all enjoying the same
blessing and I want to let you no that I hant herd from you yet I
want to hear from you very bad I dont see much satisfaction now nor
want until I here from home all thoe I am doing very well you all
mite get sick and die and me not here anything about it I hant got any
thing hardly   We here that there is some proposals for peace but I fear
that ould jef daves wont come to them it dont look to me like there
any use of fiting any longer I think they had better make peace now
then to wate til we are subjugated it looks like we cant whip no where
they whip us at every point here is shermans hole armey and nobody
to fite them only a few cavalry and a few militia and it takes the

cavalry all the time to watch the movements of the army the boys is
all well I will send this by one of my regiment ther is several of the
regiment got detail to go home after horses   I cant rite but little but
I think if I could get a letter from you I think I would rite a heap
more I would love to see you and no how you all are getting on and I
would love to no what people think about the war we here that tennessee has gone back in the union[175] and georgia is trying to go back
two   Mariah when manuel gets done holling you mite let some good
hand have one of your mules to work for his feed   there is a captured
nego here that I could by if I could send him home but I dont see no
chance[176] nothing more only I remain your affectionate husband and
friend til death

John W Cotton

Southcarolina Camps near   Cartonville[177] February 1st 1865
dear wife again I take my pen in hand to rite you a few more lines to
try to let you no that I am well and all our boys Asa and billy brown
is bowth riting we will send these letters by one of the regiment I hope
these few lines may find you all well and enjoying yourselves as well
as possible I hant got but little to rite to you there is a rite smart of
the regiment getting furlows but I dont see any chance of me getting
one   I dont no what to rite without I would get a letter from you I
hant got nary one yet there was fore come to our regiment last nite
but nary a one from our settlement home sweet home   how I long to
here from home but would rather bee at home we have moved camp
since I rote before the yankeys are advancing there scouts were in 7
or 8 miles of here last nite we are falling back as they advance towards
augusta I dont no where we will take a stand to fite them we may
take a stand soon and we may not take a stand this side of augusta I
here that general wheeler said we would have armistis in less than ten
days but I dont no whether he said it or not we here a heap about
peace[178] but we dont no whether to believe it or not but I would be

175 A convention of men, most of whom had fought on the Union side, held a
meeting early in January at Nashville to reinstate Tennessee in the Union. Parson
William G. Brownlow was elected governor.
176 How slow human beings are to learn the meaning of what they know. In this
letter he admits (as he had done earlier) that the Confederacy was whipped and
he knew that meant freeing the slaves.
177 See above, January 20.
178 Peace agitation had continued throughout the war in most sections of the
Confederacy but organized effort was especially strong in Alabama and Georgia.
Coulter has a good chapter on the subject (*Confederate States,* chapter XXII).

glad if it was true nothing would do me more good than anything else
for themto make peace for I want to come home very bad for I dont
want to spend all of the best of my life here in this cruel and unholy
war but I hope to outlive it so I can once more enjoy freedom again I
·daont no what else to rite now I must stop riting for the man that is
going home is hollowing for the letters nothing more your affectionate
husband til death

John W Cotton[179]

179 Here the letters end. Nothing specific is known about Cotton's war experience
after February, 1865, except that he was paroled at Talladega, Alabama, as a
prisoner of war, May 25, 1865 (Edward F. Witsell to Lucille Griffith). We do
know, however, about the activities of the Army of Tennessee to which the 10th
Confederate Regiment belonged. What was left of Hood's command was moved
east to Newberry, S. C. via Columbus and Milledgeville, Georgia, and on February
23 Hood gave up his command. On February 24 General Joseph E. Johnston was
again placed in command and morale rose. In early March he entered North Carolina, going by different routes towards Goldsboro. Near there, on March 19, he
fought the Battle of Bentonville, the last victory for the Confederate army.

Sherman's army outnumbered Johnston's four to one and on the 21st Johnston felt
compelled to retreat in spite of dashing cavalry skirmishes of the day. On April 9,
the very day Lee surrendered, Johnston reorganized what was left of his army but
on the 14th he surrendered to Sherman at the Bennet farm house near Durham.
(Horn, *Army of Tennessee*, 419-428; Davis, *Rise and Fall of the Confederate Government*, II 680-685; DuBose, *Wheeler and the Army of Tennessee*, 456-470; Sherman, *Personal Memoirs*, II, 268-380; Upson, *With Sherman to the Sea;* 155-162).
The 10th had 300 men when it surrendered (Brewer, *Alabama*, 693).